MAKE THEM LOVE YOU

Kevin Malachi Cullen OSA

MAKE THEM LOVE YOU

VERITAS

Published 2001 by
Veritas Publications
7/8 Lower Abbey Street
Dublin 1

ISBN 1 85390 577 1

British Library Cataloguing
in Publication Data.
A catalogue record for
this book is available
from the British Library.

Cover design by Bill Bolger
Printed in the Republic of Ireland by Betaprint Ltd, Dublin

Veritas books are printed on paper made from the wood pulp of
managed forests. For every tree felled, at least one tree is planted,
thereby renewing natural resources.

THANK YOU!

A lady named Philomena tackled my horrific manuscript and turned it into a thing of beauty and a joy forever; Philomena – a lovely Grecian name, meaning 'beloved lady'. Beloved Lady, with all my heart I thank you!

I thank, too, Mr Joseph McCarroll for his many suggestions, and above all for lending me so much of that precious commodity, his time. I may not say 'Beloved Joseph, I thank you', but thanks just the same, Joe.

CONTENTS

AUTHOR'S NOTE

What drives a tired old man to sit down and write his story? With me, I suppose, it was the endless questioning of my sister's grandchildren, curious about me, a Stone Age person, just home from Africa. Their questions stir up a ferment of buried memories.

'Kevin, did you ever shoot a lion in Africa?'

'No, I never did.'

'Kevin, in Africa did you ever kill a snake?'

'Enough, you scallywags! It's an hour past bedtime. Off you go!'

They go, and I sit pondering. The memories continue to ferment, deep down, clamouring for life . . .

1

THE RED ROSE

'Let's go for a walk,' my father said, taking Dermot and me by the hand. It was a sunny Sunday morning after Mass in June 1924. Dermot was seven, I was nine. We had just come from Enniscorthy to live on our ancestral farm in Ballytarsna, south Wexford.

My father led us down a leafy lane to a paddock where rabbits scurried for cover and a few sheep lifted innocent heads. He stood still for a while, gazing on a long, low mound dappled with daisies. At last he said, 'That is where I was born . . . And my father. And his father before him, back, back, nobody knows . . .'

We were silent, sensing his mood. At last I asked, 'What happened?'

'The evictions of 1888,' he said. 'My father stood by Parnell and Davitt. He refused to pay the back rents. So the police came with their rifles and the bailiffs with their battering ram. My father was the strongest and the gentlest man in the parish. He planned to go quietly. But when he saw the savage way they threw out the furniture and the delph, breaking things, he went for them. He wrestled four policemen around the kitchen till they beat him over the head with their rifle butts and threw him out on the grass in his blood. Here, at your feet.' My father's face twisted and he turned away. I saw the thing happening: the fight, the shouting, the terror of the children. I saw the battering ram, three tall poles with a tree trunk slung beneath them. I heard the crash as it struck the side of our house, and the thud as great pieces of the wall fell inward.

'How old were you then, Dad?'

'I was seven. Willie and Julia and Anna were older.'

'Your mother, she must have been sad . . .'

Again his face twisted. 'My mother died six months later of heartbreak and misery. Come.'

He led us further down the lane to where our land joined the Red Bog. We were in a little field choked with furze bushes, their yellow blossoms blazing in the sun. 'This is where we lived after the evictions. The neighbours helped us build a temporary house. But it was fifteen years before my father got his land back. Here, my mother died. From here we went to school until we grew up and scattered . . . Willie and Anna went to America. Julia became a nun in Kenya. I was apprenticed to the printing trade in Wexford town . . .'

'And your father?' I asked.

'He was alone. He turned to building labourers' cottages. When I was your age I drew sand from Duncannon Strand to Mullinderry with a red jennet. Sand for plastering. When he got back the land he built the house we live in now.'

We moved among the clumps of furze, pondering. I was the first to see it: a red rose lifting its head above the golden furze, hemmed in but triumphant. We breasted our way into it. It was a royal rose, red-purple, with a delicate fragrance. My father came out of his trance, grew excited even. 'This was the front door. Right here. There should be periwinkle here too.' We searched and found it, its blue trumpets muffled by grass but still sounding their silent song. Standing there, my father blessed himself and was silent, as in a holy place.

In silence we moved back to the new house. To me, the red rose was the symbol of all the buried pain we had sensed that day, lifting its head in beauty year after silent year, waiting for a human hand, a human voice. It stood for all the ruined homes of Ireland, places sanctified by the lives of those who lived and loved and suffered there. Here they prayed and worked out their salvation, and cried to God with salt tears when the evil day came, and grass covered the little paths worn by the children's feet, and briars invaded the hearth stone. I have a fancy that when all things are made new, these holy places will be restored in some form or other. There, the family may meet again with love and laughter, and ponder on the why and wherefore of the olden sorrows. Then may they turn and gaze with love on the Rose of all roses, and blush in the light of her answering smile.

The Rebel

From the place of the rose my father went to school and won the prize for the best attendance. The prize was A. M. Sullivan's *The Story of Ireland*, a story that glorified our past. Brian Boru was there, sitting on his horse at Clontarf, the Cross upraised as he exhorted his troops:

> *Stand ye now for Erin's glory.*
> *Stand ye now for Erin's cause.*

Sarsfield was there, stricken at the Battle of Landen, his heart's blood dripping into his cupped hand as he murmured, 'Would that this were for Ireland!'

Emily Lawless was there with her 'After Aughrim':

> *She said, ten times they fought for me,*
> *Ten times they strove with might and main,*
> *Ten times I saw them beaten down,*
> *Ten times they rose and fought again.*

Inevitably my father became a fierce patriot. The Saxon must go. Ireland must be free and Gaelic. *Gan teanga gan tír* was his slogan. In 1900 he began to learn Irish in the Gaelic League in Enniscorthy. In 1907 he wooed and wed my mother, Martha Purcell. In 1913 he listened to Pearse's impassioned speech on Vinegar Hill, urging Enniscorthy men to join the Irish Volunteers. Three hundred did. When Dublin rose in Easter Week they raised the flag, drove out the police and awaited the enemy attack, ready to make a new Thermopylae! As it happened, the Rising was over before the enemy arrived. The rebels were rounded up and interned in Frangoch, Wales, where my father taught Irish to his comrades.

On their release they resumed the fight. My father had the rank of Commandant in the Volunteers. One night when he was sleeping at home, we heard the crash of rifle butts on the door and the sound of alien voices. The Black-and-Tans had come for him. They took him, roughed him up and interned him in Spike Island, where he finished his war.

Then came the Truce, the Treaty and the Civil War. Fellows who had not shown their noses while the Tans were here began to swagger about with Webleys on their thighs. Each side begged my father to join them. He refused, disillusioned and sick at heart. Old comrades became bitter enemies. He had literally staked his life on Ireland Free, Gaelic and Noble. His dream was shattered. The death of Collins and Griffith broke his heart.

He decided, unwisely, to leave the town he loved and, like Horace, to seek peace on his Sabine Farm. He transferred from the *Enniscorthy Echo* to the *Munster Express*, commuting by rail to Waterford. And that is how, on a sunny Sunday in June of 1924, we found the Red Rose.

Innocent in Eden

For all of us, I think the dearest place is the place where we played as tiny children, new-minted from our mother's womb. Our house was in Bellefield, in fields outside the town. One field sloped down to a water-cressy stream overhung by Scotch pines that were always sighing in the breeze. Flowers grew there, and tall rushes that made secret hiding places. The girls, Mairéad and Eva, Eithne and Eimer, made daisy chains and played girls' play, while Dermot and I squatted in the stream, catching sticklebacks in jam jars until our bottoms were cold and soaking wet. There was no before and after to those days, only a joyous Now as in eternity. The sheep nibbled and bleated and shared our paradise, all innocent in Eden.

We began our schooling with the Sisters of Mercy. Sitting with my comrades in the High Infants, I gazed on a gothic window, the grace of its slender arches, and on the blue and white statue of Mary. A vase of mauve tulips stood before her, their chalices half opened. I gazed as unreflectingly as a sheep, and beauty stole into my heart. It is good for small children to have lovely things to gaze on. To be sure Van Gogh's *Sunflowers* would have been lovely in their way, but of the earth, earthy. The image of Mary and her tulips had a heavenly dimension that fed our spirit: Mother, Mother of God, Mystical Rose, Morning Star. The cadences of her Litany clung about her. Our May Altar at home was another fount of beauty. Eimer, being the youngest, crowned Mary with flowers on the first day of May. Each of us had his or her jam jar filled with bluebells, buttercups, daisies and hawthorn, which we placed at Mary's feet. Each of us said his or her decade of the Rosary. For the sake of the little ones my mother shortened the ten

Hail Marys to five, and sang a little verse in between. Even now, the sudden sight of bluebells in a wood or the scent of lilac after rain brings back the murmur of those twilit Rosaries and a waft of Mary's presence.

God blesses us in many ways. After my mother, my greatest blessing was to have had Sister Patrick with the soft brown eyes as my teacher. She was, my mother said, a Miss Joyce from Graiguenamanagh. She prepared me and my comrades for our First Communion. All I can say is that she passed on her own precious faith to us, a faith clear and strong as death. She was a true handmaid of the Lord. May she be blessed eternally.

The Young-Eyed Cherubim

'Buff will be the priest,' our Aunt Anastasia used to say. Anastasia, a good old Grecian-Wexford name, meaning 'resurrection'. We shortened it to 'Stasia' or 'Sta'. I was Buff, so called because of my passion for the stories of Buffalo Bill Cody. Why she picked on me, rather than Pat or Dermot, I don't know. But there it was, 'Buff will be the priest'. But Buff had a mind of his own.

For my eighth birthday I received a white shirt, patent leather shoes and corduroy pants of electric blue. I was the bee's knees, and I knew it! Our house and the house opposite were the only ones on this stretch of road. Each had its back to the road. I stepped out of our garden gate and stood in the shade of a sycamore tree that overhung our wall. The sun blazed on the white dust of the road, on the white wall of the house opposite and on the dandelions that ran like melted butter along its base.

I glanced at its garden gate. Three steps led up to it and an arch of roses spanned it. Nobody there. I stuck my fists in my pockets and strutted up and down our footpath, whistling. It was a rather windy whistle, for I had only just learned how to do it. But it was O'Neill's March that came out, no doubt about it. Up and down I marched, with a right-about and back again, the white dust spurting about my feet.

Suddenly she was present: a small girl in a yellow frock, newly come to live there, and her name was Flo. She stood under the rose-arch, gazing at me with great wonderment. I pretended not to see her. But

O'Neill's March waxed stronger, carrying quite across the road. Tramp, tramp, went my patent-leather feet, puff, puff went the dust, louder and louder waxed the March. There was battle-fury in it now, and marching hosts and the death of thousands. The girl gazed on, solemn-eyed, twisting the hem of her frock.

Then a voice called 'Flo, come into your tea', and she was gone. O'Neill's March continued, but now with a note of great and lonely sacrifice on high mountains. Then came my call to tea, and the music died, and the hosts vanished, and I sat into my tea like any little boy. 'Buff will be the priest,' Aunt Stasia said. Little do our elders know what goes on in the minds of their young-eyed cherubim!

The Silver Trout

Our mother often said, 'Pray always, for when we stop talking to God, someone else starts talking to us.' We knew who that was.

One day Dermot and I caught a little silver trout. We put it in a barrel of water at the end of the house, and were adoring it when mother came by. 'Watch its gills,' she said, 'In-out, in-out. What's it doing?'

'Drinking water, Mammy.'

'If you take it out, what happens?'

'It will die.'

'It's the same with us,' she said. 'We live in God, just as the trout lives in water. And we must drink in God, the way the trout drinks in water.'

'But, Mammy, how can you drink in God?'

'By praying,' she said 'when you say little prayers like "Jesus, Jesus, Jesus" you are drinking in God, his love and grace.'

That evening she taught us a few of her own little prayers. The Holy Name was her favourite. 'The name of Jesus is honey for the heart and medicine for the mind,' she said. She taught us, 'Jesus, my Lord and my God . . . Jesus, my God, I love you . . . Mary, my Mother, pray for me', and so on. Tramping my way through many parts of the world since then, I have said them to the fall of my feet. I still do.

My mother's people were Protestants. In the 1860s three sisters used to drive into Enniscorthy from Scarawalsh. They were known as the Three Handsome Pierces. The youngest of them, Peggy, fell in love with a Catholic farmer named Willie Purcell, handsome and gallant, a sweet singer of songs. Great must have been her love, for she became a Catholic to marry him, even though her family disowned her. Like Ruth, she may have said, 'Where thou shalt dwell, I also will dwell; thy people shall be my people, and thy God my God.' She was my mother's mother.

My mother brought up her ten children with patient love and suffering. The only remorse I feel for my past is that I did not show her enough love while she lived. But what son does? We leave it until it is too late. In Deansgrange cemetery near Dublin, there is a poignant epitaph. It contains one word only, carved large and deep into the limestone: MAMMY. That says it all.

Bleeding Roots

In 1924, as I have said, we left our beloved town, where every boy had his dog, his pigeons and his 'Vinegar Hill linnet', sweetest of all singers; where old ladies sat gossiping on their doorsteps, wearing a man's cap and smoking a *dúidín* upside down; where old men, sitting on Pigmarket Hill, would point across the Slaney Valley to Vinegar Hill, where, on the rock face under the tower, when the sun was right, you could see three priests in black vestments, forever offering Mass for the souls of the men of '98.

Moving home is like transplanting a flower. There are bleeding roots. Mother and children – even the little dog and cat – feel it. My mother parted with the friends of her girlhood, friends in whom she could confide and have a laugh and a giggle. A laugh and giggle can assuage a lot of pain. She never complained.

My father soon realised that he had made a mistake in moving. He did not find the peace he sought. We town-bred children were not made for farming. Besides, there was no secondary school nearby. After five years he sold the farm and set up his own printing establishment in New Ross.

We children made the most of our years of country life. To the sober locals we were exotics, speaking Irish, singing and dancing, wearing kilts and going to Feiseanna, where we won first prize as the Best Irish-speaking Family in the County. We were proud to be of the O'Cuilliun clan, who had dwelt here, as the poet said, 'before the coming of Christ'. Cardinal Cullen was one of us. They intermarried later with the common Cullens, who arrived only with the Normans, and our ancient name died out.

Our parish was called Tintern and our parish priest was Father King, tall, dark, delicate, remote. Father Ned Doyle, who reigned in Gusserane, was ruddy and rustic and jolly. He kept a few cattle 'to have a drop of milk for my tay'. Father Isaac Scallan was thin, ascetic and shabby, travelling in all weathers on his bicycle, a holy man. Father Hugh Kinsella of Poulfur was holy in his own way. He entertained the Travelling People, gave them a place for their caravans, cut their hair and prepared their children for Holy Communion. If they were hungry he gave them a share in his own supper of yellow stirabout in a black pot, with milk.

Everyone in the parish went to Mass, all except Jack Doran. Jack had come home a bit shell-shocked from the war. The boys asked him one day, 'Jack, don't you go to Mass at all?'

'I don't then,' said Jack, 'But mind you, the Mass is wholesome.'

Dream-time

The children are after me again with their questions.

'Kevin, when you were a boy there was no TV or anything. How did you live?'

'True, there was no TV. No electric light even. We chopped sticks for the fire and went to the well for water. Just like St Patrick or Brian Boru. And we did our 'ekkers' by the light of an oil lamp.'

'Kevin, what were you like as a boy? You, yourself.'

'Well, if you want to know, Cormac Mac Art asked his dad that very question two thousand years ago. And Art told him:

> I was a listener in woods,
> I was a gazer on stars.

'I was a star-gazer too. I used to stand in the Red Bog at night, smelling all the smells, feeling the moths brush against my cheek and hearing the jacksnipe make his moan, up there among the stars.'

I do not tell the children that this made me very forgetful, and that my father used to explode and say, 'You'd forget your head if it wasn't tied to you.'

My tenth and eleventh years were my dream-time. I wandered the land, just wandering and pondering, standing by rushy streams, at one with the flowing water. I lay down on an ancient path and pressed my cheek to the grass, reaching out to my ancestors who walked and talked here long ago. I laid my hand on the great stones in hillside fences, touching the hands of ancient men who had put them in place. The past was as real as the present.

At this time Dermot and I were reading *Old Celtic Romances* and *Finn and His Companions.* We relished the battle of the Fianna against the King of the World, down there on Ventry Strand – how Oisín put his finger through the loop of his spear and made a cast that transfixed the foreign King. We greatly desired to have spears.

Now my father had planted a circle of fifteen fir trees, a sacred grove in memory of the fifteen leaders executed after the Easter Rising. And what could make a better spear than a slender fir tree peeled? We were tempted, and we succumbed. We cut down two, covered the butts with moss, made our spears, and thank God our father never noticed.

In Ballytarsna now, in my old home, there lives a boy named Tomás Walshe. A year ago I told Tomás the story of our evil deed. Since then Tomás, having a keen sense of history, has planted two new trees to make up the sacred number. God bless him!

Besides dreaming, I enjoyed working on the land with the local lads, thinning turnips, making hay and following the threshing engine. For thinning turnips we bound sacks around our knees and legs with binder twine. When the soil was soft it was pleasant to move along the drill with a few companions, discussing the ways of the world. When the call came for the 'four o'clock tay', we went to the headland, with every herb that grew clinging to the clay on our knees. We sat against the ditch, ate our brown bread and drank our mug of tea, then read the greasy paper the bread was wrapped in.

My father, in later years, retired to Enniscorthy, where his fellow-citizens honoured him by making him Peace Commissioner. My mother, too, had a laugh and a giggle once more with her girlhood friends, Emily Nolan and Frances FitzGerald. My father found peace at last and became convivial. As his glass was being filled he would murmur, 'Pour forth we beseech thee.' After the first, tentative sip,

'Cause of our joy'. Then, after a deep, satisfying draught, 'Ahh, comfort of the afflicted!'

Father and mother, they were laid to rest under the 'plain of crosses' near the River Slaney, beside their beloved children, Dermot and Mairéad. There, too, lies the aunt who used say, 'Buff will be the priest'. And there lies the youngest of the Three Handsome Pierces, my mother's mother, beside the man she loved, Willie Purcell, sweet singer of songs.

Requiem aeternum dona eis, Domine:
Et lux perpetua luceat eis.

Wexfordmen

On my first day in Ballycullane school I sat between Lar Kehoe and Pat Nolan. Lar was the strongest and gentlest of boys; Pat was ruddy and brown-eyed, handsome as a girl. Lar grew up to father eight sons, who formed the nucleus of the famous Boley Tug-o-War Team, world champions many times. One of them, Martin, won the World Ploughing Championship three times.

I parted from Lar and Pat in 1928, when I went to college. Pat, after working a few years for the farmers, joined the British Army. Thirty years later we corresponded, Pat being then with the BAO in Hamburg. He wrote:

> I was in Singapore when the Japs came in the back door and took us all prisoner. I was one of a working party of 650 officers and men sent into New Guinea to build roads. When the war ended and we were rescued, out of the 650 there were eighteen survivors, and Staff Sergeant Pat Nolan, of Ballycullane, was the senior surviving officer! . . . I have never forgotten the Faith that was instilled into us in school. In Hong Kong, in 1958, my wife and I started the Legion of Mary. We were only five miles from the Chinese frontier. Within a year we had a warrant officer ready to join the Faith, and fifteen Chinese members of the Army Fire Brigade under instruction. Did you ever meet that great lady, Edel Quinn, in Africa?

God be with you, Pat Nolan. You ended your life as a Chelsea pensioner. Ireland gave you nothing but the Faith and you kept it honour bright.

One other boy I must mention from those days. He was Mikie Furlong, a natural warrior, with red hair and blazing blue eyes. From the beginning he and I bristled, and our bristling ended in an epic fight that began at lunch-time and continued after school. Sixty years later, revisiting the little village, I asked about Mikie.

'Mikie Furlong? A hard-working man. A bit crippled now by a fall from a horse. His wife Alice died last year. Mikie drives up to the cemetery every morning and stops at her grave. He says the Rosary, sitting in the car, then into the half nine Mass.'

I watched Mikie enter the church and take his seat. I sat in beside him and murmured, 'Push in there, Mikie. You did not win that fight.' He turned to me, his face pensive with prayer, and gazed for a long time. Suddenly the blue eyes blazed. 'Oh, by the hokey! It's *you!*'

We had good talks for a couple of summers until Mikie went to sleep beside Alice his wife. A man poor in possessions but rich in nobility, a *duine uasal.*

In summer holidays, Dermot, Ethna, Eimer and I used to drive in the pony and trap to Bannow Bay. For long, sunny hours we paddled and swam, speared flat fish with our mother's two-pronged fork, and gorged ourselves on cockles, which we loved. Then ashore, to pick blackberries to assuage our thirst, and so happily home in the gloaming. Nobody worried or asked, 'Where were you?'

Once, cousins of ours, the three Fitzharris girls, were overtaken by darkness on the way home. When they came to the Cross of the Three Gates, which was haunted, they got down and put their hands on the ass's back for protection. Everybody knew that the cross on the ass's back was holy. It was there because Jesus had sat on it, entering Jerusalem.

In Love

When I was twelve I began to cycle to the de la Salle school at Ramsgrange, six rough miles away. If God had blessed me as a small boy by giving me Sister Patrick as my teacher, he blessed me again by giving me Brother Charles. One day he sat on a desk, hitched up his cassock and read us the life of Guy de Fontgallant, a saintly French boy of eleven, who died in pain, loving God with his whole heart. His story made me want to be a priest. Aunt Statia's prophecy took a tiny step forward.

The tyres of my bike were old and patchy. I had to pump them up every so often and, remembering my mother's words, 'pray always', with every stroke of the pump I used to say, 'Jesus, Jesus', or 'Jesus my Lord and my God'. I was, therefore, a good boy? Maybe a holy boy? Don't make me laugh! Every boy is like the moon: a dark side and a bright side. I leave my dark side to God.

When I was thirteen, inevitably, I was in love again. After all, of all the lovely things there are in life, the loveliest is to love and to be loved. Her name was Kathleen, and she lived in a paradise by the sea called Arthurstown. To me she was pluperfectly beautiful, with blue-black hair, truly violet eyes, slender as a wand and full of devilment. On Sundays I used to cycle down to her place, ostensibly to swim with her brother Cyril and partake of her mother's tea and seedcake. Did she love me? I don't know, for I never told my love. But we used to engage in that delicious parley of the eyes, where every glance rings loud as thunder on the heart, and souls commingle.

Cycling home on the white roads at dusk, rejoicing in the scent of woodbine and the blast of a melodeon from some cottage door, I was filled with an exaltation that comes but once in life. At the end of that summer of 1928 I went away to college in Dungarvan. Kathleen, in due course, joined the missionary Sisters of Our Lady of Apostles. But we shall meet again, Kathleen, for I trust in the words of the Hound of Heaven:

> *All that thy child's mistake*
> *Fancies as lost, I have stored for thee at home.*
> *Rise, take my hand, and come.*

Into the Rough

In St Augustine's College, Dungarvan, my days of wine and roses were over. Trapped in a swarm of noisy boys, one had to stay alert. I sat beside one Finnegan, who used to mooch about, moaning:

Be-cause I nevah haddah gal,
That's why I wanna gedda gal.
Another sang, *'Yes, we have no bananas'.*
And a third: *'Climb upon my knee, Sonny Boy'.*
Songs that were strange to me who had been weaned on *Boolavogue*.
City lads swapped pictures of their favourite film stars.

Mary Pickford was mentioned, and Greta Garbo and Gloria
Swanson. Limerick City lads I found a little aggressive – they still
showed the fighting spirit that had thrown King William back from
their walls in 1690. The only fight I was forced into was with a
Limerick lad named Larkin.

A tiny argument in the handball alley led to a challenge to fight. I
did not want to make an ass of myself before a gang of boys, and said
so. But Limerickmen had their own battle ritual. A chap named
Fanning held up a straw between Larkin and me, intoning: 'Who *daar*
spit over that?'

Larkin spat, not only over it but on it. Fanning cast it dramatically
on the ground – the battle-gage. Larkin picked it up, and with a
contemptuous flick of his fingers, struck me on the cheek with it, the
coward's blow. Well, what could one do? I thought of Cú Chulainn:
'Better short life with honour than long life with dishonour.'

Coats off, sleeves up, a ring was made and seconds appointed. For
two or three rounds we boxed in a gentlemanly way. Bare fists, of
course. In the third round, hearing a deep voice among the boys, I
thought a teacher had caught us, dropped my guard and turned to
look. It was only Jack O'Neill, a big boy from Knockanore, the Hill of
Gold in west Waterford. But in that split second Larkin's hard fist
crashed into my right eye. I truly saw stars, red stars, flocks of them.
At that my diffidence vanished, my battle-fury arose, and that was the
end of it. Larkin collapsed. As we went to seek balm for our wounds
we became the best of friends. I believe that Martin Larkin, of Wolfe
Tone Street, Limerick, subsequently became a priest in South Africa.

We played rugby in winter and hurling in summer. Hurling was my
love – the hero-game of the Gael ever since Setanta made the longest
solo-run in history, carrying the ball on his stick from Dundalk to
Armagh, then shattering the pampered lads of King Connor when
they ganged up against him!

In our dress we were foppish. The cult of the hanging-out shirt tail had not yet arrived. The 'in thing' was to wear Oxford bags, wide-as-possible flannel pants with a knife-edge crease. We preserved the crease by folding the pants under the mattress each night, between two sheets of brown paper. Only the bank clerks wore plus fours, the ultimate in style, if not beauty.

Brooks of Vallombrosa

The best thing I got out of St Augustine's was a love of English literature. Mr O'Hara was a magical teacher. I have seen boys come to him from haunts of coot and heron, the turf still adhering to their boots, and in a week or two they were quoting Shelley around the schoolyard. George Kiely was an ex-pupil of his who became a reporter on the *Dungarvan Observer*. I remember Mr O'Hara's joy when George proclaimed to the nation that, 'The pot-holes on the road between Dungarvan and Kilmacthomas lie thick as autumnal leaves that strew the brooks in Vallombrosa!' Great stuff!

He taught Greek with equal zest. If you wished to leave the room he commanded, 'The password, Sir!' And you gave the password of the Greeks at the Battle of Marathon: 'Zeus, Sother kai Niké!' – Zeus, Saviour and Conqueror. I achieved notoriety in my Intermediate exam by getting high marks in everything, but in maths, only 18%. I therefore failed the whole exam. That was me! The following year I concentrated on maths and, with the help of the Thirty Days Prayer, passed my Matric.

At the end of our college days, three of us felt the urge to be priests. Why me? Many of my comrades were better men. They felt not the slightest urge. Why me? Some extra goodness in me? Stop! I was not good. Did I hear a voice calling? No. Did I feel a sweet attraction? No. Just an urge. In later years a professor told us: 'Don't ever feel proud. It may be that God called you because he knew that otherwise you would have damned yourselves.' Too true.

Three of my school comrades received their Final Call before they were twenty. Tuberculosis, the scourge of those days, swept them off. They were three noble youths, truly *daoine uaisle*. I name them here: Willie Hart from Roscarbery, Humphrey O'Donoghue from Kenmare, and David Mary Alexander O'Shea from Kilmallock.

A few years later the same enemy swept off my beloved sister and brother, Mairéad and Dermot, the noblest of our family. They died, yes, but they live. Standing beside the grave of Lazarus, Jesus said to Martha: 'Have I not told you that if you *believe*, you will see the glory of God?' Then he cried out in a loud voice: 'Lazarus, come forth!' And the dead man sprang into life.

To Orlagh

In 1932 I and eight other boys entered the Augustinian Novitiate at Orlagh. It stands in the foothills of the Dublin Mountains, out Rathfarnham way. The first thing we were asked to do was, 'Write down why you want to be a priest'. I wrote down what I felt, six words only: 'I want to be near God.' Later on I found that King David had had the same thought three thousand years before and put it in a psalm: 'To be near God is my happiness.' It is a fact of life.

The Augustinians took their origin from St Augustine, the brilliant intellectual of Roman Africa, a contemporary of St Patrick. In a book he called his *Confessions*, he tells of the wasted years of his youth when he 'barked like a dog at the Catholic Church', and of his fierce joy when he found Christ. In old age he summed up all his wisdom in one famous sentence: 'You have made us for yourself, O Lord, and our hearts are restless till they rest in you.' 'Made us for yourself', meaning orientated towards yourself as a flower towards the sun, and needing you as a flower needs the sun. Without you, we sicken.

To signify our new life, each of us was given a new name. Mine was Malachi. Henceforth I was known as Mal instead of Buff. I was sorry to lose my old name. It fitted me.

'I'm supposed to turn you into little Augustines,' our Master said with a sardonic smile. He did his best, with prayer, lectures, reading and manual work. 'I hope at least to make you men of discipline, obedience and humility,' he said. 'Men of prayer who will cling to Christ, come what may.'

We all found the morning meditation hard, thirty minutes on our knees, pondering on the Gospel of the day. A Cork boy gave up early on. He said to me, in a sweet Cork lilt, 'Ah, I was getting great sweetness out of the meditation early on but latterly I'm getting no sweetness out of it at all.'

My Heroes

For me, the best thing was having the world of the saints thrown open to me. My heroes were the Little Flower – she was everybody's hero – and Father Willie Doyle. Willie Doyle was the heroic Jesuit chaplain of the First War. For eighteen months he walked calmly through the mud and blood of the battles of the Somme, Ypres and Loos, ministering to his beloved Irish boys, until he too fell. I quote from one of his many letters to his father:

The Somme, 11 October, Mass for the Dead
By cutting a piece out of the side of a trench I was just able to stand in front of my tiny altar, a biscuit box supported on two German bayonets. God's angels, no doubt, were hovering overhead, but so were the shells, hundreds of them, and I was a little afraid that when the earth shook with the crash of the guns, the chalice might be overturned. Round about on every side was the biggest congregation I ever had; behind the altar, on either side, and in front, row after row, sometimes crowding one upon the other, but all quiet and silent, as if they were straining their ears to catch every syllable of that tremendous act of Sacrifice – but every man was dead. Some had lain there for a week and were foul and horrible to look at, with faces black and green. Others had only just fallen and seemed rather sleeping than dead, but there they lay, for none had time to bury them, brave fellow every one, friend and foe alike, while I held in my unworthy hands the God of Battles, their Creator and their Judge, and prayed him to give rest to their souls.

Ypres, 10 August 1917
A sad morning. So many dreadfully wounded. As I knelt beside one dying man, he opened his eyes and said, 'Ah, Father Doyle, Father Doyle, thank God'.

He motioned me to bend lower and put his arms around me and kissed me. It was all he could do to show his thanks that he had not been left to die alone. So often the Last Anointing eases their bodily pain.

A few yards away I saw a hideous, bleeding object, a man with his face smashed by a shell and both his eyes torn out. I took his bloodcovered hands in mine as I searched his face for some whole spot to anoint him. He raised his head as I spoke. 'Is that the priest? Oh, Father, Father, thank God! I can die happy now.'

So often my tears splashed down on the patient faces of my poor suffering boys.

Seven days later, on the terrible 17 August at Ypres, having ministered all day to his boys in a storm of shells, his own turn came. He was recommended for the VC, but it was denied him, his biographer says, because he was Irish and a Jesuit. Why he was not recommended for the Church's VC beats me. Who was a saint and martyr if not he?

As the novitiate year passed, we did our best to stumble nearer to God. At the end, we made our three promises to God – to live poor, pure and obedient. Then, when the others went to Rome to continue their studies, two of us were sent to University College, Cork, to do a BA.

Depression

In the university I chose English and Philosophy as my subjects. I honoured especially Daniel Corkery, Head of English, Dr James O'Mahony, Head of Philosophy, and Dr O'Rahilly, biographer of Fr Willie Doyle. In my third year there, depression settled on me like an atomic cloud. We four students lived in St Augustine's, Washington Street. The priest in charge of us was dull and unimaginative. Our sole recreation was an hour's walk in the city. We marched two by two, in uniform – black suit, black hat, white collar; always on parade, never in civilian clothes. Touchers trotted after us, whispering, 'Father! Father!'

No games. That was the worst. In May '36 I watched, from my high window, the lads and lasses in open-necked shirts, heading off to the Lee Baths or the hurling field. A great stone settled on my heart.

For summer holidays we used go to our old college in Dungarvan. Surely it will pass now, I thought, with swimming and mountain climbing and whatnot. But no. It stuck. My parents came to spend a week with me. My mother sensed there was something wrong, and as we parted she whispered, 'Remember, if you want to come home, you're welcome.'

Strange to say, I never thought of leaving. In the end, I broke the chain that bound me in my own way. On a sunny day in August, a student named Frank Geary and myself stood on the college roof. In the distance, beyond various gardens and houses, we could see the orchard of the Convent of Mercy. One tree bore red, red apples that shone brightly in the sun. We talked of orchards we had robbed as boys. Suddenly Larry said, 'I bet you wouldn't rob that orchard!' Just as suddenly I knew that this I must do. This deed, foolish, disobedient and a little mad, would lift the stone from my heart.

The Cure

At 3 a.m. I donned rubber shoes and a black pullover, slipped past our Master's door, trotted downstairs, opened a window and dropped into the first garden, then the next and the next and the next, until at last I came to Moloney's coal-shed, huge and high. I swarmed up a pipe, up and over the roof, and now I was looking down on the nuns' garden. How far was the drop? I hung by my fingers a while, wondering, said 'ach' and let go, and landed on a bed of lilies.

Turning around, I saw the little white crosses of the dead nuns glimmering at me through the gloom. I said a prayer for their souls. Then I went to where I had marked the tree with the red, red apples, and plucked three only. After that I mooched about for an hour or two, savouring the hell of it. I looked up at the windows of the sleeping nuns and prayed for the souls of the dead nuns until dawn whitened the east. Then I thought, suppose the Reverend Mother had spotted the intruder and rung Sergeant Dan Regan! I fled, climbing and clearing various sheds and walls like a greyhound, and so to bed.

I slept; I woke, and the stone was gone from my heart. I presented Frank with the magic apples. Why a little deed of derring-do like that should free me, I don't know. But it did.

In the autumn of '36 I finished with UCC. The last question in my last exam was: 'It is hardly fair to say of Kant that he considered the mind to be a kind of machine-shop, whose function was to impose order on the undifferentiated manifold of Reality. Discuss'. I discussed, and said farewell: my next stop was Rome.

To Rome

To date I had studied many things, often unwillingly. But I felt a frisson of excitement at the thought of studying theology, the science of God, the ultimate Reality. I knew that people had always sought to know who were the gods behind the gods, what was the reality behind appearances, what was the secret heart of the universe. Some said one thing, others another. In their wildest dreams they never dreamt that the secret heart of the universe was a Sacred Heart, that it was made by love and for love. Now I was about to study the mystery of the One who not only made it, but lived in it, the most fascinating Person who ever walked the world.

I knew that he had revealed himself ever so slowly in the books and history of the chosen people. When at last he came it was not as one would have expected, with a clash of cymbals that rang from heaven to earth, but softly softly. As the medieval poet put it:

> *He came all so still*
> *Where his Mother lay,*
> *As dew in April*
> *That falleth on the spray.*

He came all so still, and the name he took was gentle: Lamb, the gentlest of all creatures; Lamb of God, who takes away the sins of the world.

I began to study in the Gregorian University. The Jesuit Fathers were my teachers, and my comrades came from every corner of the earth. The German students stood out everywhere in their scarlet cassocks; a punishment, it was said, inflicted on their forebears, who were too fond of the Roman pubs. All our lectures were in Latin. We Irish, with our blunt minds, envied the Latins their razor-sharp minds, the Spaniards, the Italians and the South Americans. They could syllogise, distinguish and sub-distinguish *ad infinitum*.

We studied hard, prayed hard and played hard. Thursday was our free day: we were free to visit the art galleries and the glories of ancient

Rome, or to play football. I chose football, since my heart was set on the foreign missions. We of the Augustinian College played soccer against the Scots' College, Gaelic against the Irish and rugby against the English College. I played wing-forward in rugby, a position I relished.

I was surprised to discover how much theology we had learnt from our Primary School catechisms of long ago. We knew full well that God was not One Person, a lonely Eye in the Sky, so to speak, as the Jews and Muslims believed. We knew that he was more like a Family – three distinct Persons bound and bonded together in an infinite furnace of love, and a unity of being, beyond our conceiving. Three Persons co-equal and co-eternal, sharing the one divine nature. We knew that, though we could not put it into those words.

God Is Love

Now I was to learn what brought this glorious God down amongst us. St John told us. He said simply, 'God is love.' And, as I knew well, love tends to overflow, to give itself. So, from eternity, it seemed, God had decided to create us lot, so that he could love us, and we him (even for God, the loveliest thing in life is to love and to be loved!). But he knew that inevitably we would make a mess of things, would prefer a hell of our own making to his heaven. He knew, too, that the only way to gain us for himself was to become one of us, to take all our sins and sorrows on his own back, as if he were the guilty one, and to die for us.

He did so. He thought it worthwhile. Without ceasing to be God, he became man. We duly crucified him. We crucified God. He died of love. Until we meet him face to face, we shall never understand his incredible love and humility.

The Men of the East

There was a book about these things that I loved. It was called *De Verbo Incarnato*, Concerning the Word Made Flesh.

It dealt largely with the men of the East whose subtle minds, Greek-Oriental, were fascinated by the Man who was God. They got their mental teeth into him, tugging this way and that.

When St Patrick brought us Irish the Gospel of St John and we read, 'In the beginning was the Word, and the Word was with God, and the Word was God . . . And the Word was made flesh and dwelt amongst us', it was enough for us. We believed. We accepted Jesus as truly God and truly human, and we worshipped him. Then we went about the serious business of bringing the Good News back to a barbarous Europe (it was European scholars, not ourselves, who later called us the Island of Saints and Scholars).

But the men of the East had unquiet minds. They questioned everything. Was Jesus truly God? Did he exist from eternity? Was he truly human? Or, 'since matter is intrinsically evil', had he only a phantom body? Had he a human soul like us? Had he a human will? . . . A divine will? . . . Two wills? . . . Was he one person only? Or two persons loosely joined as one? Could Mary be called Mother of God? . . . Or mother of the human Jesus only? . . . Yes or no?

'Was Jesus God or not?'

So they went on, often in error, while Rome as ever was the anchor of truth. One Arius, a subtle Egyptian priest, taught that God the Son was glorious, divine – but not quite God! There was a time when he did not exist . . . So the Jesus who died on the Cross was not God . . . So we were not saved . . . Arius put his doctrine into ballad form and it spread like wildfire. The Army took it up, then the nobility, then the new barbarian Christians, newcomers. Battles, then wars, were fought over it. Had the Arian doctrine prevailed it would have been the end of the Christian religion. But a General Council of the world's bishops was called at Nicaea, a town in Asia Minor. There the Pope's Legates and the assembled bishops prayed, deliberated and, with the help of the Holy Spirit, hammered out the truth about the Person of Jesus Christ. Like cut stone upon cut stone they built truth upon truth in the Nicene Creed that we repeat every Sunday at Mass. They proclaimed that Jesus is: 'God from God, Light from Light, true God from true God, begotten, not made, of one Being with the Father. Through him all things were made.' 'Of one Being with the Father' – that was the capstone that nailed Arius. To put it shortly, Jesus is one Being with the Father, therefore perfect God, just as he is one Being with us, and therefore perfect human.

The Nicene Creed is the greatest body of truths ever assembled, and the greatest song ever sung. I sing it myself every morning rising:

Credo in unum De-e-e-um (I have a lovely voice, even if it sounds terrible). At night, for a pillow-prayer, I say the exquisite,

> *O King of the Friday*
> *Whose limbs were stretched on the Cross,*
> *O Lord who did suffer*
> *The bruises, the wounds, the loss,*
> *We stretch ourselves*
> *Beneath the shield of thy might,*
> *Some fruit from the tree of thy passion*
> *Fall on us this night.*

Who is she?

Suddenly the spotlight shines on the little girl of Nazareth, so humble, so innocent, so strong. 'Who is she that cometh forth as the morning rising, fair as the moon, bright as the sun, terrible as an army set in battle array?'

She is Mother of the One Person who is truly God and truly human. May we not therefore call her Mother of God? Oh yes! Everyone suddenly burst out singing, 'Holy Mary, Mother of God!'

But a great voice bellows: 'Stop! Silence! You cannot call Mary Mother of God. In Christ there are two Persons, loosely joined, the divine and the human. Mary is Mother of the Human Person only. So you cannot call her Mother of God.'

Consternation! It is the voice of Nestorius, great Bishop of Constantinople. Even he can fall into error and out of the Church. Tens of thousands follow him. As ever, Rome is the pillar and the ground of truth. Pope Celestine calls a General Council at Ephesus in the year 431 – he who sent St Patrick to Ireland in the following year. Again the bishops gather and pray and hammer out the truth, that Jesus is one Person. 'Much as the soul and body make one man, so God and man make one Christ, and Mary is his Mother, so, we may call Mary Mother of God.'

The Ephesians were delighted. They formed torchlight processions and surged about the city all night, singing over and over, 'Holy Mary! Holy Mary! Holy Mary, Mother of God!'

Every day in our prayers we call Mary Mother of God, and never think of the battles that have been fought through all the wild centuries to preserve the Truth.

'Tu es Hibernicus?'

'Buff will be the priest,' Aunt Stasia said. Yes, but I nearly fell at the last fence. The texts for the last exam before ordination were *De Verbo Incarnato*, Concerning the Word Made Flesh, my favourite subject, and a dry little book about Minor Orders, namely the steps that, formerly, led up to the priesthood. They were Porter, Acolyte, Lector, Sub-deacon and Deacon. I revelled in *De Verbo* and never opened the dry little book.

But it was from that dry little book only that the examiner shot questions at me. Blank . . . Silence . . . I tried to explain Silence . . . At last, with a long, sour look, he said, *'Tu es Hibernicus?'* You are an Irishman?

'Utique, Pater.' Yes Father.

'Mm! Saltem haves fidem?' At least you have the Faith?

'Utique, Pater.'

He was a little Sicilian, willing to bend things a bit. 'Look,' he said, 'if you swear to study this material during the holidays, I'll let you through.'

'Utique, Pater! Gratia, Pater! Mille, mille gratia!' God bless him!

I was ordained in July 1939. On that day I wrote to my Provincial volunteering for Africa, and on the back of my Brieviary I wrote this little poem from the Gaelic:

> *I give my soul to you, O King of the Sunday.*
> *Never, never, shall I ask it back.*
> *You are my witness, O Queen of Mercy:*
> *I have left my soul forever with your Son.*

The best thing I got from my studies was a simple, yet a big thing: a just appreciation of God, his humility, his love and pity, that he is the God of Allowances. The preachers of my childhood had given him a bad press: his love was veiled. Now the force of his second name stuck into me: Lamb, *Lamb of God*, not Lion. The story of the Prodigal Son in Luke 15, where the gentle father received back his rascally son with such pity and love, was a character sketch of God. That, said Jesus, is what God is like. A glimpse of this is more precious than silver and gold.

'Go and teach'

In 1938 Rome had granted a mission territory to the Irish Augustinians. It was in the bush country of Northern Nigeria. I had volunteered to go there. Years later a snooty lady asked me, 'Why must you go and force your religion on these people? Haven't they got a religion of their own?'

'Madame,' I said, 'do you believe that Jesus Christ is God?'

She began to dither. 'Well,' I said, 'I do. And the last command he gave before he left this earth was, "Go and teach all nations, baptising them in the name of the Father and of the Son, and of the Holy Spirit . . . And know that I am with you always, yes, to the end of time." For me', I said, 'those are Standing Orders, given by God and never cancelled. Finish!'

In August '39 Germany invaded Poland. In September, England and France declared war on Germany. In the spring of 1940 the university was half empty: English, German, Austrian, French, Dutch, Italian and Belgian students were called home. On Good Friday 1940 Mussolini attacked Albania. France fell to the Germans in June.

Mussolini declared war on France and Britain from his balcony in the Piazza Venezia. The Romans listened to him in dead silence. They remembered what war was like. We Irish got home to Ireland in small groups via Lisbon. My group crept up through Biscay in a tiny Irish boat, showing no lights, and so to Dublin.

I was put teaching students. I had a passionate love of Gaelic language, music and literature, which I indulged to the full. I began to put down roots, deep roots. Then, in May 1942, the bell tolled. A ship was ready to leave for West Africa. I went home to New Ross to say goodbye to my people.

My father said, 'What possessed you to volunteer for Africa in this war?'

I said, 'Dad, what possessed you to turn out in Easter Week?' He laid his hand on my shoulder and that was all.

It was hawthorn time, heartbreaking for beauty. At the May Devotions they were singing 'Bring flowers of the fairest' and the tune built a nest in my heart. I cycled about saying goodbye to everything, with an undercurrent of pain at the beauty that cannot be held. But it's all the same in the end, I felt: if we grasp too eagerly at beauty we may lose it, whereas if we give it up, we somehow hold on to its essence. A strong old Wexford patriot of my father's day lifted my heart. Saying goodbye, he took my hand and said, 'Young man, Wexford is proud of you.' Wexford is proud of you! It meant a lot to me. There was a clang of '98 about it.

The day came. My mother said goodbye only with her hand and her eyes. I thought of Pearse's poem to his mother:

> *Lord, You are hard on mothers,*
> *They suffer in our coming and our going.*

With my brothers and sisters I went out to catch the bus for Dublin. Just then there came the sound of music, and the Corpus Christi procession came along the street, band playing and banners flying. As we knelt on the pavement, the people all smiled and waved goodbye, and the King blessed me as he passed. He knew. It was a good start.

2

ON THE WAY

From Dublin, on a June morning in 1942, with two comrades long since dead, I set out for Belfast, thence to Stranraer, Glasglow and the Clyde. There we were asked to declare the goods we carried in a huge wooden crate. So green were we that we had no manifest. 'Open it up.'

Fortunately we had bought a box of tools in Lenihans of Capel Street. We opened up and displayed saddles, bridles, Mass kits, shotguns, helmets, delph and camp beds. We passed, reassembled the crate and went on board. There we met a dozen other missionaries, SMA and St Patrick's, Kiltegan men. We sailed out and joined a convoy of about a hundred other ships. They were carrying tanks, guns and ammunition right around Africa and up to Egypt for Montgomery's build-up against Rommel. The passengers were all soldiers and civilians, no ladies. Our last glimpse of Erin was of the hills of Donegal, far off, sunken in the sea.

West, then south we sailed, to avoid subs and planes. The corvettes raced around the convoy, dropping depth charges here and there. We picked up a boatload of torpedoed sailors. A depth charge blew up on a corvette, killing a sailor. At sunset the whole convoy hove to on a glassy sea. We saw the flash of the flag as the body was committed to the deep, a moving moment.

At last our ship peeled off and turned into Lagos. From Lagos we travelled 500 miles in a creeping train to Jos, thence another five hundred miles in a Mammy Waggon to Yola, our HQ. A Mammy Waggon is a great lorry piled high with goods, on top of which the passengers perch precariously. To the owner, his lorry is a splendid Argosy, brightly painted and named. Ours was named 'In God We Trust'. Another was, rather grimly, 'Rem. Your 6 Feet'. We arrived at Yola on 15 August 1942, the feast of Mary's Assumption into heaven.

We had arrived. What did we hope to achieve? We knew not. We had faith, hope and courage. We would try. Fifty-five years later, in a spurt of anger, I was driven to proclaim what we did achieve. Here is what happened.

The Canard

In September 1997 the *Irish Times* carried a headline: IRISH MISSIONARIES RUIN INDIGENOUS CULTURES. It then quoted a Canadian professor, lecturing in Ireland, as saying: 'The smashing of native cultures was accompanied by criminal and sexual abuse.'

The slander annoyed me. I wrote to the Editor:

Sir

I am unacquainted with Canada. No doubt the Canadian WASPS treated their indigenous Hurons, Iroquois and Mohicans with the utmost tenderness, like the American WASPS.

What I know is that I have been a missionary in West Africa for nearly fifty years. When we went there, in war time, all travel was by horse and foot. We swam the rivers, climbed the mountains, learned the languages and taught our people the Good News: that God is a God of Love, who dwelt amongst us and died for our sins. That was very good news for them. It lifted a stone from their hearts, the endemic fear of evil spirits and witchcraft.

Meanwhile we built schools and clinics, sank wells innumerable and taught better agricultural methods. We inculturated – Africanised – the Liturgy, using the native languages and music. The professor ought to visit our Sunday Mass. For one and a half hours, with native music, song and dance, we offer sacrifice and praise our God.

Do come, professor! But no, you prefer to throw a stone and run away. One remembers the words of Fulton Sheen: 'If I were a pagan seeking the true Church of God, I would pick the one that is most hated and vilified.'

Yours, etc.

That is a fair estimate of what we did achieve over the years. But let me go back to the beginning.

Nigeria

Our Pioneers, two Irish and two English Augustinians, had come to Yola in January 1940. They were Fathers Paddy Dalton and John Power of Tipperary and Limerick respectively, and Gabriel Broder and Hugh Garman of London and Kent. Already they had built a house, a church and a school in Yola, and begun to build two out-stations. It was good going.

We new boys were brought first to sign the Resident's Book. He had to know who came and went. The Resident administered our mission territory, called Adamawa. It was roughly the size of Ireland. It was subdivided into districts, each administered by a District Officer or DO. Some of the DOs had distinguished names, such as Trapps-Lomax, Delves-Broughton, Drummond-Hay, Blair Fish and Usher-Wilson, whose father was a bishop, and Lennox-Cunningham of Ravensdale, County Louth.

At the turn of the century the British had 'pacified' what was then a medley of perhaps three hundred tribes, and called it Nigeria. For the sake of trade they imposed the Pax Brittanica, put an end to slave-raiding and war, and built some roads, schools and hospitals. The Fulanis were the dominant tribe in Northern Nigeria. These were Muslims of Semitic stock, tall, light-skinned and subtle. In a Jihad about 1820, they had harried the pagan tribes and claimed to 'rule' over them. The British found it convenient to rule the pagans *through* the Fulanis, a system called Indirect Rule. The pagans lived as their ancestors had done since Eden, independent, self-sufficient, growing their own food, weaving their own cloth, making their own tools and weapons.

At this time the war was going badly for Britain, what with the sinking of their ships and Rommel's driving of the 8th Army back to Egypt. The colonies, including Nigeria, were held by a skeleton staff, so to speak. But there was no panic. The British ruled by force of character, with a steely coolness.

To the Bush

I was appointed to go to Sugu, 105 miles away, 'under the wise guidance of Fr Broder', the Londoner. A horse was bought for me for £4, carriers and loads organised, the headman blew the three marching notes on his whistle, and off we set, single file along the bush path. Every eighteen miles or so, the DOs had had rest houses, or *Baraki*, built. A rest house was a mud hut, large, round, thatched, with a doorway but no door. A circle of smaller huts for the carriers surrounded it. A local man was appointed *Sarkin Baraki*, 'Lord of the rest house'. His job was to organise wood, water and a skinny chicken for the white man, and food for the carriers. For this service he was paid.

Each morning we rose at 4.30 to offer Mass by the light of a bush lamp, while our cook, Michael Dan, made a breakfast of coffee and bread. All went well until the fifth and last day out, when we came to the River Ine. All the rivers had been in flood, since it was the wet season. We had crossed them, swimming with the horses. All you had to do was sit daintily on the saddle and move with the horse. The Ine was in deep flood. Gabriel's horse struck a submerged branch in mid-stream and he came off, went under, and was swept away around a bend. The trouble was that he, being English, was properly attired for riding, wearing riding breeches and boots, while I, being Irish, wore khaki slacks and canvas shoes. His breeches and boots filled and made it impossible to swim. He was swept off, almost verticle in the water, struggling to keep his chin up.

'I felt my legs caught in weeds,' he said afterwards. 'I was sure I was done for then. I made a desperate plunge, got free and felt my feet touch a sandbank. I stood up and rested, up to my neck. Thank God!' We shouted to the carriers to stay where they were till the morrow. Gabriel travelled the rest of the way like Lady Godiva and suffered no more than sunburn!

Nooky Places

Next morning I woke up to hear a boy singing *Kyrie eleison* out in the corn. Gabriel had already started a little Christendom with a school of eighteen local boys.

My job was to learn Fulani, which was the lingua franca of this territory. Gabriel had already learned Hausa for use in school. I studied the grammar, then enlisted the help of a local Fulani named Haruna, illiterate and charming. There was a book of animal stories that are told all over Africa. Haruna especially loved the Story of the Monkey and the Pakkara (the pakkara is the African partridge). The story ran:

Every sunset the pakkara, as everybody knows, gives a long, sad cry, 'Duni-yaa-ru! Duni-yaa-ru!' (duniyaru means 'world' in Fulani). One day the monkey asked, 'What is this duniyaru, this world, you are always crying about?'

'Would you like to know?'

'I certainly would,' said the monkey.

'Right! Come up in this tree with me.'

They sat on a branch side by side. After a while the monkey said, 'Pakkara, I see hunters coming.'

'Be quiet!' said the pakkara. 'Soon you will know the world.'

Again the monkey said, 'Pakkara, they are surrounding our tree!'

'Don't worry,' said the pakkara, 'Soon you will know all about the world.'

'Oh, Pakkara,' cried the monkey, 'they are firing the grass around our tree!'

'True,' said the pakkara. 'Now you will know all about the world.'

And as he flew off he cried, 'Duni-yaa-ru! Duni-yaa-ru!'

And Haruna would burst his sides laughing.

On my first Sunday there I took a book and went out, seeking a nooky place in which to sit and read – you know, green shade and honeysuckle atmosphere. I found none. Hot sun burned above, hot ground beneath, and black, sharp-fanged ants attacked my bottom. The milieu was hostile. I rose and came in.

'Where were you?' my comrade asked.

'Out looking for a nooky place.'

'A what?'

'A nooky place to sit and read.'

I can still hear his guffaw. 'You daft, romantic Irishman! You didn't come out here to go mooning about in "nooky" places! You're here to do a job of work. You've got to be a realist, my boy.'

Poor me! I had assumed that all English people had a dash of Wordsworth in them, were given to wandering about in vacant or in pensive mood, drawing sustenance from daffodils, lesser celandines, rooky woods and such. 'Gabriel,' I retorted, 'you have the soul of a hedgehog. And it was your grandfather Broder who murdered Brian Boru!'

A Country Called Masassa

After four months I was fluent in Fulani. Then my boss said, 'There's a country down south called Masassa. Only two or three days' ride away. Organise carriers and chop (food) and go there. Lots of villages there. Go around and get two boys from each village. We need boarders here.'

'Boarders?' I said, thinking of colleges at home.

'Boarders. We have four good round houses built. They can eat and sleep there. Our plan is to teach them, baptise them and train them as catechists. In due course they can go home and evangelise their own people. Take the *maidoki* to look after your horse and Mike Dan to cook for you.'

Mike Dan was our general factotum. *Maidoki* means horseboy. Keeping a horse is difficult. There are no fenced fields, so you keep your horse tethered in an airy hut. To feed it, the horseboy cuts the long grass and chops it into short lengths. You give it its ration of corn yourself and watch to see that the *maidoki* does not take it home to his wife.

Trekking in the dry season is monotonous. You must adapt your pace to that of the carriers. In the cool of the morning you sing, thinking of Sarsfield or Sir Lancelot maybe. As the sun moves up, you plod along dumbly through a black and tawny land, black where the bush fires have roared over it, tawny where patches of grass have escaped the fire. Thirst and fire have trained the scrubby trees to attitudes of agony, and the mountains, burnt naked, shimmer like steel.

We arrived at Masassa and made for the chief's house. Meeting two likely lads on the way, I 'put talk on them'. Their names were Bulla and Warsu, sons of Garba and Bello. 'You are noble youths,' I said, and gave each a shiny penny.

The chief was a dignified man with a sad face. I told him my mission, and that I wished to meet the elders. He bowed and went away. I gave his son a shilling to buy three pots of beer, for every palaver has to be oiled. The elders came, grizzled men with good faces. They sat around the wall and clapped their hands in greeting. Then, remembering Livy and all the Romans, I spoke.

'O Chamba men, you are wise. You know that today the whole world is opening its eyes. The tribes around you, the Bachemas, the Verres, even the Mumuyes who dwell on the mountain tops, have opened eye and can read book. Shall it be said that only the Chambas of Masassa remain blind?'

'Is it not an honourable thing to have sons who can read and write? To have sons who can collect your Government tax and write it down with honesty, instead of strangers who may deceive you? You nod your heads. You clap your hands. All that remains is to choose two of your boys who will join the sons of chiefs who are learning book in my palace in Sugu.'

Some cried approval. They were those who had no boys. Others looked doubtful. But the ball was in. The match was on. An hour passed. The old men wriggled. Some played 'gobs' with pebbles. Others built lines of pebbles along their shins. The strain was telling. The talk fizzled out. No decision. They cast longing glances at the beer. I said, 'Please call the boys before me.'

A messenger went out and came back. No boys. They were all 'gone bush'. It was time to play my ace. 'O Chamba men, as I entered your town I spoke to two noble boys. Those boys, I said, are sons of noble fathers. Their names? Warsu and Bulla, sons of Garba and Bello.'

There was a cry of approval. Here was a way out of the impasse, victims not themselves. All eyes turned on Garba and Bello, two butty, honest men. Messengers shot out and in a twinkling Warsu and Bulla were led in, like two little Isaacs going to the sacrifice. I praised them. They scowled. I said to their fathers, 'What joy will be yours when those your sons can write down the tax money! Are not my words true, O Chief?'

'True, O Whiteman, Lion, Lord of the World!'

May I be forgiven! In a body they fell upon Garba and Bello, urging them until, overcome by weight of numbers, they yielded.

Then I said, 'Let us drink.'

They fell on the beer, but with dignity, passing the yellow calabash from hand to hand. The palaver had lasted three hot hours. Mike Dan took charge of the boys and we moved on to the next village.

The Mustard Seeds

After four days I had gathered seven boys. The tactics and the speech were the same, but at the end the speech stank in my mouth. Early on the fifth morning, when the daffodil light of dawn was drowning the stars, I and my caravan turned north for home. In my heart I sang:

> *They come back, they come back full of song,*
> *Carrying their sheaves.*

Let me tell the story of one of these boys of mine. He was small and sickly, skin and bone. I had mounted him behind me on the horse. When the other boys saw him curl up on his mat they laughed and called him Gung-gung, which is a tiny snake. Right! Gung-gung was given the alphabet to learn. To our surprise he mastered it in one day. After two days he was reading from his Primer: *Ya ba ta pa. Wa ya ba ta pa? Ba ya ba ta pa ba.* Meaning: He gave her a stone. Who gave her a stone? He did not give her a stone . . . We had found a genius. In three weeks he could read anything in the Hausa language. He became a teacher, and later District Officer. He ended as Head of Prisons in Northern Nigeria.

Why have I gone into all this detail about this boy? Because that is how we sowed the mustard seed, with labour and pain, from place to place and tribe to tribe. Jesus had said, 'The kingdom of God is like a mustard seed. It is the smallest of all seeds, but when it has grown it becomes a tree, so that the birds of the air come to shelter in its branches.'

In the beginning I almost despaired. I could never see these people believing. I thought it all depended on me, great fellow that I was. I forgot that all – but all – depended on the Holy Spirit, and that it takes time for a seed to grow. But little by little the birds of the air, the various tribes, came to shelter in the branches of the Vine. First the Chambas, then the Jukuns, the Mumuyes, the Verres, the Barres, the Margis, the Higis, the Kilbas, the Komas and others.

As I write this, more than fifty years later, the mustard seed has grown into three dioceses, served by two Nigerian and one Irish bishop, and nearly all its priests are sons of the soil. A Christendom has been founded.

'Make them love you!'

In January '44 my future bishop, Father Dalton, asked me to take over Mapeo Mission. Mapeo had had a bad history. Father John Power had started it in 1940, but no sooner had he built a sturdy cottage of mud and stone and zinc, than a bad dose of malaria sent him home. As he left it for the last time, accompanied by Gabriel Broder, he turned in his saddle and said, 'Gabriel, I'm leaving it, and it hasn't even a name! I beg you, call it Santa Maria. She'll take care of it.' For he had once been custodian of the miraculous picture of the Mother of Good Counsel in Santa Maria church, Gennazano.

Nevertheless, Mapeo fell on evil days. The people grew hostile. Men fell sick there. It lay empty. There was talk of abandoning it. Then my boss said to me, 'Will you take over Mapeo?'

'Sure,' I said, 'no trouble. Any advice?'

'Make them love you.'

'Oh yeah!'

And yet it was the best advice. I packed my loads, organised carriers, and with Mike Dan set out for Mapeo. On the way we passed the ruins of a German fort. Before the First War, the Germans had occupied this territory, and during the war English and Germans had fought it out, up and down the bush. Near the fort was a lone grave. The headstone read:

Temporary Lieutenant C. J. Hebblethwaite.
Killed in action 7th April 1916.

Mike Dan said, 'I was small boy when this man die. His name, Burkono. It mean Red Pepper, the name we call man who get hot, angry head. He stand up heah and curse the Jamians in the fort, so they shoot him in the head.'

I liked the site of Father Power's cottage. It stood at the butt of a steep mountain composed of hugh black boulders. Trees grew among the boulders. Red monkeys and black baboons played up there. When frightened, the baby baboons jumped on their mothers' backs like jockeys, while the baby monkeys clung under their mothers' tummies as they sped away. On top of the mountain, Mike told me, lived the Komas, a tough, independent tribe who despised the dwellers on the plain. Out on the plain we could see the smoke of the Chamba cooking fires rise straight into the evening sky. No one came to greet us, no man, woman or child. They were still hostile.

Bujjo

After a week I had a break. Mike told me that a man named Bujjo had been 'shot with the needle'. That means that an enemy has paid a sorcerer to put spells on a needle or other pointed object, which is then flicked by night towards the victim's compound. He is then told, and auto-suggestion makes him ill. He may lie down and die. Bujjo was lying down.

I looked through my tin trunk for 'magic'. A tin of Andrew's Liver Salts. Good! A tin of after-shave powder 'By Coty', whoever he was. A splendid fragrance! Down to Bujjo. 'Where's the pain?'

In his side. 'Smell this!' I held a handful of Coty under his nose. 'Magic' I said, rubbing it hard into his side.

Then, to his wife, 'Bring water please.' I poured a fistful of Andrews into the water. It hissed and bubbled. 'Strong medicine,' I said. 'Drink.'

He drank. I stood him up and gave him a smack on the bottom. Then, to his wife, 'Cook a chicken for him every day for five days.'

Bujjo lived and became my best friend. It was he who told Mike the reason for the people's hostility. To the Chambas, the birth of twins is a dreadful thing. Other tribes rejoice, but the Chambas believe that one twin must be the child of a demon who has impregnated the mother. If it lives it will wreak disaster on the people. But which one? No one knows, so both must die. They are smothered in a pot of ashes, and the pots are buried by running water to take the evil away. The little skulls are left visible.

Mike continued: 'When Fada Pawa live heah, the chief have brother named Barde. Barde's wife born twins. Fada Pawa say, if they kill 'em, he go tell District Officer. But they kill 'em. Then two policeman come and bring Barde to Yola. They say he stay prison for six months. But after two months he die. The chief and people blamed Fada Pawa. After that they no like Mission.' From their point of view they were justified.

Rain

There had been no drop of rain for eight months. In March the temperature climbed to 115 degrees and stuck there. The bush was dead still. 'Rain go come soon,' Mike Dan said.

Sure enough, next morning a black line lay on the eastern horizon. It climbed swiftly into towering black-purple cliffs. Lightning flashed in its dark chasms. There came a roaring sound as the wind drove clouds of yellow dust across the land. The trees sprang into a frenzy, tossing their arms, shouting to the storm, shouting to each other that the rain, the rain was coming! The dry grasses threw themselves flat on the ground and shrieked for joy; deep in the earth the parched roots felt the commotion and whispered, 'Rain, the rain!'

There came a commanding crash of thunder and white fire. A pause – then the sound as of a thousand drums rolling, coming nearer, full of menace. It was the rain. It struck my zinc roof and the continuous roar drowned out even the thunder.

I loved it, praised God for it. Mike and I came out in our shorts and danced and opened our arms to it. Ahhh! Thank God.

Next morning every Chamba – man, woman and child – hurried off to their farms. It was an atavistic urge – rain, farm, food. They passed my door but not one of them greeted me or came in. With the rain come the insects – flying ants in myriads, praying mantises, their front legs raised as in prayer, horned beatles, sausage flies and whatnot. They shake out new wings and take to flight. They see the light of my bush lamp shining on the veranda. It looks like heaven. They rush for it, flittering and fluttering. Ping! Thud! Swish! They fall to the floor in a creeping, rustling carpet.

The Jolly Frogs

Next come the jolly frogs. They drink. They swell up like balloons. They grow drunk. They begin to cheer and shout and sing. The big fellows shout, quite plainly, 'More wa-ther! More wa-ther!', while the

little skinny fellows scream, 'Gimme beer! Gimme beer!' They, too, see
my light and they come. Fat frogs, thin frogs, smooth frogs, warty
frogs. Up the steps they hop, in deadly silence now. They are hungry.
They want meat, fresh meat, red meat, living meat. The one I call Big
Warty leads them. He is a giant in rusty armour, crusted, battle
scarred. They fan out over the floor like fielders in a cricket game. A
sausage fly, drunk with light, falls to the ground. 'Gallup!' says Big
Warty. With a crackling of bones the sausage is gone. A fierce praying
mantis, a green dragon six inches long, singes his wings and zooms to
the floor like a crippled bomber. All the other frogs back away. Big
Warty plops to the attack. He scowls. The mantis rears up in fighting
pose, those terrible hooks held in front of his face like a boxer. Big
Warty jumps in, using his weight, knocks him sideways and seizes him
across the middle. There is a desperate flurry of wings and legs for a
while, then a slow crunching and cranching as the poor mantis
disappears. I feel no sorrow, for perhaps it is a Mrs Mantis. I have seen
a Mrs, when her mate had finished making love and was resting cheek
to cheek – I have seen her turn her head sideways and casually begin
to eat him, beginning with his lips. Waugh!

A dozen or so frogs kept on coming every night, and, like
customers in a pub, each had his own seat. Big Warty's was under my
chair. One night, sitting reading, I heard grunts of protest. I looked
down and saw a snake, a horned viper, a bad fellow. He had clamped
his fangs around Big Warty's left hind leg. Warty would jump forward,
the snake would pull him back; forward again, back again. I grabbed
a bamboo cane and slew the snake, but poor Warty died that night. He
may have saved my life.

Uaigneas!

The wet season set in in earnest. A blanket of cloud rested on the
treetops. The grass grew six feet high. No one came and no one went.
I listened to the hiss of rain on the leaves and the ping-ping of drops
on a rusty tin. Night after night I stood on the veranda and listened.
No sound but the chorus of the frogs. I picked up a book and put it
down. I put a record on the gramophone and McCormack's silvery
voice rang out:

I hear you calling me,
You called me when the moon had veiled her light,
Before I went from you into the night . . .

I moved outside and down the bush path. The voice followed me, thin and piercing clear. I moved on until it was but a silver thread of yearning in the night. I stopped and faced north towards home, looking up at the stars. Pale, shadowed faces of my loved ones rose before me as, charged with pain and wild regret, the last words of the song shivered through the night:

I stand – do you remember? – listening here,
Hearing your voice through all the years between.
I hear you calling . . . me . . .

Urgently I whispered the names of the people I loved, as if they were but a few feet away. Only the frogs answered. For several nights I repeated that ritual. Every man, no matter how tough he thinks he is, has his weak spot. At last I caught on to myself. 'Cullen,' I said, 'you're growing morbid. Snap out of it.' I broke the record across my knee. Too near the bone! Never again!

The Breakthrough

I prayed and prayed and prayed. I rode around the compounds picking up crawling children and saying how lovely they were. In vain! But salvation was nearer than I thought.

One day Mike appeared at the door with Bujjo and Bujjo's wife. She was holding an emaciated baby in her hands. Mike's face was full of tragedy and appeal, for his heart was tender. 'Look, Fada, this manpiccan done born five days now, and his mother's milk dry up. See, Fada, he like to die.'

The baby's head lolled back like a broken doll, and his little fists were clenched on his bony chest. 'Make we baptise him,' Mike said. We christened him Patrick, making him a child of God and heir to the kingdom of heaven. 'Good, Fada!' Mike said, 'We done fix his soul, but we no can fix his body. He mus' die now.'

'We go fix his body too, Mike, and make him proper fat piccan.'

'Fada can do this thing?'

'You go see, Mike.'

Memory is wonderful! I had just remembered that my sister Eva, she who had put the COTY in my kit, had also thrown in a couple of teats for a baby's bottle. 'My lad is finished with these. They might come in handy some day.'

Praise God, I had milk. A nomadic cattle Fulani was camped nearby and sold me a bottle a day. I dug out the teat and boiled it, while Mike boiled the milk and filled a clean bottle with three parts milk to one of water. My best guess!

Then we fed our little Temple of the Holy Spirit. His little mouth muscles had only strength to take a few drops at a time, then he would rest and pant a little. I, being fourth in a line of ten children, was an expert in feeding, though the bottle in those days was boat-shaped to keep it from rolling out of the cot.

Courage, Pat! With patience we made his little tummy swell until it was round and shiny. We laid him in a soap box then and covered him from the flies.

That was in the morning. During siesta I heard the noise of a multitude. I stepped out to find about fifty Chamba women draped along my veranda. 'Mike,' I called, 'What brings these women here?'

'They come to see Fada's Little Mama.'

'What Mama?'

'The Mama that feed the baby. They want see it with eye.'

Oh, the teat! Mama means breast. They wanted to see Fada's Little Breast! OK. We prepared the milk, brought out Sir Patrick and I began to feed him on my lap. A volley of exclamations. A clapping of hands. They clustered round us, a wall of hot flesh. I waved them back to get air for Pat. As he drank on in his little manly way, the wonder grew. Suddenly they broke into uncontrollable laughter, flinging themselves about, slapping their thighs, falling on one another's shoulders, the tears streaming down their cheeks.

'Fada's little Mama! Fad's little Mama!' they screamed.

Praise God! It was a great day. The barriers were down. Human nature had spoken to human nature. I was their brother, their sister, their mother even, doing a woman's work as well as any woman. At the end of the week I saddled up and went into Yola for supplies. While there, I had a letter from Mike.

'O my Father, a bad thing has happened. I am afraid to informing you. I rem. your words, "Watch that Little Mama well and boil it every time". This very morning I do so. I leave bottle ready on kitchen floor. I go outside to make palaver with some man. One minute only I am absent. When I return I meet three goats, they rush out against me from kitchen. Within I see the bottle lying. The teat the goats have eaten. The milk is scattered. O my Father, my heart cry out. It is the only teat in all the world. The women come today to see. In vain. I feed Patrick with spoon. Forgive me, O my Father.'

Poor Mike! Next day I sent him a new teat. I returned to find Pat hale and hearty and the women still in kinks of laughter. 'Make them love you', my boss had ordered. Now they did, and, as everyone knows, the loveliest of all things is to love and to be loved.

The Chamba Women

Let me say something about these Chamba women. They are butty in build and jolly in heart. Leaves are their vesture. Just as Adam and Eve, finding they were naked, 'sewed for themselves fig leaves' to cover themselves, so do the Chamba women. They have a girdle round their waist from which depend bustles of leaves, one before, one behind. Dressed thus, they are perfectly modest. There is nothing erotic about breasts; they are simply for suckling infants. In fact, the first hint of eroticism came twenty years later among the Mumuyes. From Lagos a cargo of bras percolated up-country: In due course some Mumuye maids came forth, clad in the beauty of peach-coloured bras. The same maidens used to play a kind of hurling at the beginning of the wet season, with curved sticks and a large nut for a ball. So the then incumbent, Fr Moore, organised a match between the Bras and the Non-bras. Never before was there such a match, and never will be again.

The Non-bras won.

One good thing about the Chambas is that they hate hatred and love good relations. They believe that sheer malice can cause physical evil such as illness or death – and who can say they are wrong? They dread evil spirits that hover around like flies and must be placated by sacrifices. They dread witches, who may be men or women, and can cause the death of children. In my time there, two male witches had their throats cut in a nearby village.

The ancestors, too, can be kind or unkind. A young married woman named Fanta had never conceived. Both families held a pow-wow. Yes, it was true, Fanta had once insulted her granny, now dead. Granny's resentment must be the cause of her barrenness. So Gongwori, the village priest, offered the sacrifice of a white cock to placate granny's spirit. In vain.

The families assembled for another pow-wow. Perhaps one of Fanta's living relatives held malice against Fanta? No; they all said they loved her. Were they telling the truth? To find out, Gongwori placed a few grains of corn on Fanta's head and held a white cock over it – white, the colour of light. If the cock picked a few grains, all was well. If not, someone was still holding out. The cock did pick a few grains. And, as a matter of fact, Fanta did conceive in due course.

After the breakthrough with the baby's teat, I wooed Gongwori. He became my friend. When he saw me coming he would cry out, 'Mona-me bari!' – My friend has come! He allowed me to watch him offer sacrifice for a sick child. It was like this:

A year after death, the Chambas remove the skulls of their fathers and place them in a sacred grove. I went there with Gongwori and his little son, Musa, who carried a white cock. The ancestral skulls were in a pyramid six feet high by eight at the base. Those at the base were crumbled away with age. Gongwori squatted and prayed: 'Spirits of my fathers, do not be angry with me for calling you. I pray for the sake of the child Misa, son of Jatau, son of Bobboi, son of Gongputsa, son of Gongshemen . . .' Back into the mists of time he called their names. Then he killed the cock and gave it to Musa, who circled the skulls, sprinkling the blood over them. When I asked Gongwori afterwards why it was Musa who sprinkled the blood, he said, 'I am a sinful man. My little boy is innocent.'

The Good News of God

Now the children began to visit me in the evenings to hear *Labarin Allah,* the News of God. They were my delight. Of all the happy things to do, for me the happiest is to teach children the News of God. Already they knew God. They called him SU. They knew he was Lord and Maker of all things. They knew he was good. But he was far, far away, while the spirits were near, and had to be placated by sacrifice. They were happy to hear from me that God was a God of Love, who dwelt amongst us and died for our sins. Happy to know that if we call on him we need never more fear evil spirits and witches. Their hearts were wide open to grace. A picture of Jesus crucified cut them to the heart. They sighed and murmured, 'Sorry, Jesu! Sorry, Maria! We repent.'

I had one more job to do, and that was to learn the Chamba language. There was no grammar, as it had never been written down. I had to learn it because I am certain that people can never really pray except in the language they drew in with their mothers' milk. I took it by storm. For seven to eight hours a day, using relays of boys, I kept at it. The boys already spoke Fulani. By dint of asking the word for this, and how to say that, the language grew into me. It was simple and sweet, spoken with a Kerry lilt.

In due course I turned the prayers into Chamba. Then the Question-and-Answer Catechism. Then hymns, some to Latin melodies and some to Chamba. The Sisters of St Peter Claver in Rome printed them for me in one neat book. Our little Christendom had begun to bloom. Christ had caught up with his Chambas – after how many centuries? As many as there are since the Garden of Eden! The Nailed Hand was reaching down to caress them at last, and the Holy Spirit was shining in their hearts.

Stones That Cry

One evening I asked my children, 'Would you like to build a house for God?'

'Oh yes, Fada. We boys can dig clay, the girls can draw water, and we can all trample it into mud, to make blocks.'

Good! I paid Bujjo and two comrades to bring small rocks from the mountain for the foundation. Next evening no children came to hear *Labarin Allah*. The moon was well above the trees. I rang my bell again, the steel axle of a lorry. It shivered up to the stars. Still no children.

Next day I asked Juguda why? He was King of the Boys. He fidgeted, then said, 'We felt fear, Fada.'

'Fear of what?'

'Fear of the big rocks. They were crying in the night.'

'Why were they crying?'

'They were crying after their little brothers that you took from them.'

'Who told you?'

'The old people.'

'Did you hear them cry?'

'We heard, Fada.'

'How did they cry? Like what?'

Juguda made a long-drawn-out sound, half sigh, half moan. 'Like that, Fada. Like a man crying after his children. The big rocks were lonely.'

'But stones cannot cry, Juguda. They have no mouths.'

'True, Fada. But they *know*. They can converse, like trees, or like the wind.'

It was the primeval intuition that the universe is alive; that there is a dim consciousness, a 'soul' in everything. The Greeks felt the presence of dryads in the trees and naiads in the streams. To the Chambas the mountain is alive. I remembered now, at the height of the wet season, when the rains had loosened a hugh boulder that came crashing down like thunder over the village, the old men had come out with their flutes and, moving in a circle, had played a gentle, soothing kind of tune, such as would put a child to sleep. 'The mountain is angry,' they said. 'Someone has done great wrong.'

Like the Greeks, they too felt that human crimes outraged Nature and caused storms and earthquakes.

I realised that I, too, must have hurt the old men's feelings when, on Sunday afternoons, having no one to talk to and no place to go, I used climb the mountain and send the odd boulder bounding down, smashing trees on its way. The brutal whiteman! I repent.

But I have more empathy with my Chambas than with horrid Western man who sees a soul in nothing; to whom the earth is only a thing to be raped. No sacredness. No God, even. I think of Wordsworth, so long ago, deploring our crudity in a poem:

> *The world is too much with us. Late and soon*
> *Getting and spending we lay waste our powers . . .*

Our Church

In spite of the Crying Rocks, we got our church built. It was round, made of mud block, eighteen feet in diameter, and plastered smoothly with worm-casts, which abounded there. It had a conical roof of golden thatch and its walls were whitewashed inside and out. A lime-white mansion! I had cunningly mixed Reckitt's Blue with the whitewash, to give a cool, blue tint. Lovely!

But, I ask you, what is a church without a golden tabernacle and a rose-red sanctuary lamp? It looks empty, uninhabited. Therefore I, for once far-seeing, had procured a tabernacle and a rose-red lamp from the Armagh Apostolic Workers, God bless them! (Apostolic Workers are groups who supply missionaries with vestments, chalices and so on.) My church had a mahogany altar, but no benches, for my children could sit on mats.

I planned to make the opening of the church a state occasion. The Government unwittingly helped me. It was May 1945 and the war was over. The Resident was sending out messengers to announce that the King of the English had beaten the King of the Germans, and was therefore granting £3 to every school to celebrate the victory. Fine! I too received £3, a magnificent sum in those days, when a day's wage was fourpence. I told the Chief and people that we would thank God with prayer on Sunday morning and a feast in the afternoon.

Mike Dan and I were the only two Christians. We planned to bring the Blessed Sacrament from my house and install it in the new church. Mike led the way, clad in a long white alb and carrying the Cross. Next came the children, carrying holy pictures in split canes and singing my hymns to the tap of the drum. After them came the multitude. And lastly, very beautiful to see, came the Old Ladies in a phalanx, wagging their leafy bustles to the music. 'Ave, Ave, Ave Maria' went the singers. 'Wag-wag, wag-wag, wag-wag Maria' went the bustles. God bless them all.

I came last, carrying the Blessed Sacrament under a canopy made of a bedspread and four poles, festooned with flowers. I sang an open-air Mass in Latin, and delivered a sonorous sermon on how this day, for the first time, God had walked through their town. The vestment I wore that day was light as woven moonbeams. A lovely lady had worn it on her wedding day. Then, 'What shall I do with it?', she said. Her good angel made her think of me! So she drew patterns and snipped and sewed and changed it into a lovely vestment that prays for her at Mass every morning. As I remarked somewhere, it is lovely to love and to be loved!

But I digress, and my people are impatient. I tell Mike to unveil the beer – there are twenty pots and a mound of rice. I retired to the church and sat in the cool and was happy. I gazed with love on the white walls, the golden door and the rose-red lamp. Mapeo was no longer empty. It had a Heart, for He was present. The poem of an ancient Irish hermit rose in my mind, and I said it softly:

> *Grant me, O son of the Virgin,*
> *A hut in a lonely place,*
> *With only you for company –*
> *No better comrade on earth!*
>
> *A lovely wood around it,*
> *Shelter for singing birds:*
> *Blackbird, cuckoo and thrush*
> *To sing their psalms with me.*
>
> *A lovely church – O glory!*
> *Bright with lime-white walls!*
> *Fit dwelling-place for my God,*
> *For the Sweet Sacrifice a temple.*

Are we Catholics mad?

I am certain that the devil is far busier than we think. As I sat there in perfect peace, strange thoughts invaded my mind. They came from nowhere. Am I not mad to believe this impossible thing? That Christ is present here in person . . . That he changes a piece of bread into his living self . . . Preposterous!

Why do I believe it? I suppose because he said it and he is God. If he is not God it is all rubbish and I am a fool to be here. But yes, I do believe he is God. The One who at the beginning said, 'Let there be light' – and there was light. The One who, when his friend was dead and buried four days, commanded, 'Lazarus, come forth!' – and the dead man sprang into life.

So, when he takes bread and says, 'This is my body', it is hard not to believe him. I know that he wanted the Jews to believe, for he gave them a sign: he fed the 5,000 people with five loaves and two fish in the wilderness. When they followed him to town next day, he told them, 'You follow me only because of the bread I gave you yesterday. You would do better now to seek the bread from heaven.'

'Lord, give us that bread always.'

'I am the bread that came down from heaven. And the bread I will give is my flesh, for the life of the world.'

Not unnaturally the Jews ask – just as I would ask – 'How can this man give us his flesh to eat?'

This man does not draw back. He insists all the more: 'My flesh is real food, and my blood is real drink. He who eats my flesh and drinks my blood has eternal life, and I will raise him up on the last day.'

The Jews have had enough. They spit on the ground and walk away. He lets them go. Rather sadly, he turns to the Twelve: 'Will you go too?' In other words, if you don't believe, you may go.

Peter is aghast. Leave the Master? Never! 'Lord, to whom shall we go? You have the message of eternal life and we believe. We *know* you are the Holy One from God.'

Good Peter! But did you see *how* Jesus could do this thing? No. Not till the Last Supper, when Jesus took bread and said, 'Take this, all of you, and eat it. *This is my body, which will be given up for you.*' This, for me, is the sticking point. Peter and his comrades and the millions of Catholics since then believe the unthinkable, that Jesus changed bread into his living self and empowered the Twelve to do likewise: 'Do this, in memory of me.'

Do I really believe? It's easier to believe that it's all imagination. Preposterous! Can I really believe the incredible? So easy to say No . . . Sitting there, I grow afraid. I cry for help, 'Jesus, help me! I believe, Lord, help my unbelief!' I repeat that many times and peace comes back, little by little. Yes, Lord, I do believe the incredible, with your help. My faith, I know, is a gift from you. Your greatest gift. If I am mad, I am mad along with you.

The boom of the drums wakes me from my musing. The Dance is on. The sound of revelry rises higher. Wine rejoiceth the heart of people. The drums boom, the flutes flutter and men and women burst into a full-blooded Chamba dancing song. The drummers and flautists form the hub of concentric circles. Around them swirl the maidens, singing, as is their wont, an impromptu song, then the men, then the women and children. The maidens sing the solo and the rest repeat the refrain, dipping and circling with joy. The refrain they sing today runs:

> *Su Andarah, Su Andarah,*
> *O wari hande wuro min.*

Meaning:

> *Our God above, our God above,*
> *This day has come into our town.*

There is a psalm that says, 'Sing a new song to the Lord'. Today my people have begun to sing a new song. May they sing it all the way to eternity!

3

THE SPROUTING OF THE SEED

Clonmacnois

'There is a tide in the affairs of men', said Shakespeare, 'which, taken at the flood leads on to fortune.' My tide was rising. I built five round houses to hold five boys each, and three cornbins to hold their food. I rode to the outlying villages, making my classical speech, and acquired twenty boys. From the SMA Fathers in Jos, I got a teacher qualified to teach in the Hausa language. From Delves-Broughten, DO of Yola, I got permission to open a school. My boys cooked their own meals in black pots set on three stones. Thus, when I came back from my rounds in the twilight, my place resembled Clonmacnois, the twinkling fires surrounded by my disciples with books bent to the flames, droning out their lessons. One of them nearly took my head off, though. He had strung a rope between two round houses to dry his shirt on. As you know, a horse nearing his stable breaks into a gallop. The rope, invisible in the twilight, caught me under the chin, and only a quick backward twist saved my head.

I got a Yola tailor to make my lads khaki shirts and shorts, to be worn only on Sundays and market days. This finery made the Muslim youths jealous and they threatened my men in the market. So I slung a bag of sand over a branch and taught them to punch straight and hard. That settled the Town v. Gown trouble.

My boys, naturally, were hedonists, free spirits, used to their own way. I had to teach them discipline, softly softly, or they would all run. Misa, for example – his job was to chop the long grass for the horse into short lengths. He chopped a pile and then placed it just out of the horse's reach. Clever fellow! I gave him a clip in the ear and with the dawn he was gone.

Juguda was my Head Boy, rugged and strong, a man of integrity. Musa, Iya and Jidda were his lieutenants. A blast on my hunting horn at 6 a.m. brought the boys tumbling out. They lined up for orders:

'Juguda, take horse and go for milk.' (A Fulani had settled with his herd two miles away, to my delight.) 'Musa, get three boys to bring water. Iya, two boys to dig holes for trees. Jidda, take the rest, with hoes, and weed the groundnuts.'

We grew most of our own food, guinea-corn, sweet potatoes and groundnuts. Guinea-corn, which grows twelve feet high, was the staple diet of the people and mine too, for it made a strong, nourishing porridge. Noticing that the girls gathered leaves in the bush every day for cooking, I asked them to bring me some. One kind I found to be rich in oil and pleasant to the palate, and that solved my 'greens' problem.

The boys washed and had a light breakfast at 7.30, and then school from 8 a.m. till 1 p.m. I taught religion and maths myself. After school they rested and had their midday meal, while I took siesta. Around 3 p.m. we resumed action. The boys worked on the farm for an hour, then played football. At 6 p.m. I rang my bell, the lorry axle, and we entered my little white church with its golden tabernacle and rose-red lamp. There we said a short Rosary – only five Hail Marys, divided by a verse of song. Then a little instruction, followed by Benediction of the Blessed Sacrament. The way I felt was, since Our Lord is present, let's see him, let's sing to him, let's touch him with our hearts and get his blessing. It was that daily Benediction that gave my boys the Faith, strong and clear as a diamond.

After their supper they came in and sat around me on the cement floor. This was our best hour. I taught them hymns and the Latin of the Mass, and told them stories of saints and martyrs. The story of the Ugandan boys and men, who chose to be burnt alive rather than abandon their Saviour – all twenty-five of them – moved them to tears. I had translated the Big Catechism of three hundred questions into Chamba, and we talked about what we had done that day.

Chamba Lore

They, in turn, taught me the Chamba lore, as that the Sun is God, the Moon is his wife, and the Stars are their children. And did I know why some people are black and some white? Because God began to make people by day, and continued into the night – and those of the day were white, of the night black.

They all belonged to different, exogamous clans, each of which had its totem, or guardian animal. Juguda was of the Deer clan (as were the Ossory people in ancient days: they were the *Os-rige*, meaning deer-people). Juguda told me the story of how his clan became linked with the deer.

An ancestor of his went out hunting. Night fell, so the hunter climbed a tree. When the moon rose, a troop of deer appeared, doffed their skins, turned into a bevy of beautiful maidens and began to dance. The hunter crept down and stole a skin. Came the dawn. They all donned their skins, all but one poor weeping maiden. The hunter took her home, hid her skin in the thatch, married her and begot a daughter.

One day, when the hunter was at the market, the deer-lady found her skin, soaked it in water, donned it and became a deer again. The hunter came home, drunk as a lord, and fell into a drunken sleep. The deer-lady came dancing and prancing around, the little daughter tried to wake her father. In vain: the deer-lady trampled him to death and ran away.

The little daughter grew up and married and became the ancestress of Juguda's clan. He has deer-blood in him, and may never harm a deer.

One day I told that story to Professor Delargy, the folklorist. He grew quite excited. The same story was told in an ancient Gaelic, except that it was seals who shed their skins and danced. The seal-maiden who was caught and married became the ancestress of the Conneely clan of Connemara – the only family in Europe whose totem animal is remembered: *an rón*. A fishy story? Well, the Professor told me!

My First Fruits

The time had come to baptise my first boys, the first of their tribe to be Christians. All my striving had been for this. I had tried to make them know God's immense love for them and to help them return that love. From love would come faith – as Newman said, 'We believe because we love.' The evening Benedictions in my little white church, face to face with Jesus, had fostered faith and love.

Precious to the farmer are the first fruits of his crop. Precious to me were the first fruits of my teaching. Three of my boys were ready for baptism: Juguda, Iya and Musa. I prepared them for it by a week's retreat, sending them up the mountain each day, each boy to a different spur, to pray and think and be alone with God.

15 August, Mary's Assumption, was the day. The people gathered and, having put the boys' parents in front, I spoke: 'O Chamba people, today three of your sons will be made sons of God. It is Jesus, the Son of God, who will do this. You do not see him with your eyes, but he is here amongst us. You will see me pour the Water of Life on the heads of your boys. But it is Jesus who will baptise them in their hearts. What will he do for them?'

'He will wash away all their sins. He will send his own Spirit, the Spirit of God, to live in their hearts. He will give them New Life, a share in his own God-life. You three mothers, you conceived these three boys, did you not? You gave them man-life, did you not? – Yes.'

'Now listen. In this Washing, Jesus will give your sons a share in his own God-life. That will make them children of God, members of God's own Family. They will have a right to live in God's House in Heaven. And, just as you fed them on your milk to keep the man-life alive in them, so Jesus will feed them on his own body to keep his God-life alive in them.'

We began the ceremony. As the water splashed on each boy's head and ran down his face, the women burst into that thrilling African paean of joy, made by trilling the tongue against the palate. We had Mass then, and the boys received their First Holy Communion, the living Lord Jesus Christ, our Saviour and our God. They were in a daze of happiness. Juguda, now Peter, summed it up. *Fada, muna jin dadi!* We feel sweetness in our hearts like a fire. Oh, Fada, if only we could die today!'

I, too, felt sweetness. It was my third breakthrough. The first was the saving of baby Pat with the teat; the second was the procession, Mass and feast to celebrate the victory of the King of England over the King of the Germans, and this was the third. From this day everyone desired to receive 'baftisma', as they called it. These lads were my first fruits, my Golden Apples; the first Christians of all their tribe, my mustard seed to sprout in new places. They had come to me two years before with wild and fiery hearts. Today they were made new men, grafted on to Jesus by their baptism, new branches on the Vine. Praise God!

The Jug's Troubles

A week later the Jug led a deputation to me. 'Fada, we need your help. I feel shame to say this, but we are having bad thoughts.'

'But bad thoughts come of themselves. They are only temptations.'

'But, Fada, we are children of God. It is not right that we should ever have bad thoughts. Jesus said, "Blessed are the pure in heart".'

I explained that baptism does not take away temptations. But it gives us power not to consent to them, and then there is no sin. But the Jug was not quite happy. He assumed that baptism should have made them angelic in body and soul.

Soon after this, I missed him from Mass and school. 'Where is Juguda?'

Mike said, 'He get four wives, Fada, so he run away.'

'Four wives? How? Why?'

Mike enlightened me. 'His senior brother done die, Fada, and he leave four wives. Chamba law say that if a man die, his junior brother must inherit his wives. Yesterday they come to Juguda's house with their mats and cooking pots. They said, "Now Juguda, you be our man. You be our massa. We go love you and work for you all time".'

Horrified, the Jug had fled to a distant village where he lay low until other men had absorbed the four ladies. Had he accepted them he could have become a rich man, having eight hands to work for him! That's the worst of being a Christian!

'Go fall in love'

My boy Juguda was rising eighteen. 'Jug,' I said, 'it's time you looked around for a wife. But, beware. Don't fall in love with a girl just because she has light skin and a pointy nose. Or with one who is always throwing herself at boys. Go for a solid, dignified girl. Consider how she works on the farm. Consider her parents, especially her mother. Tomorrow I shall dress you in a toga, so that you may go to the dance as a man, not as a boy.'

The Jug looked very solemn at this, and went away without a word. Next evening was a dance evening, for the moon was full. I dressed Juguda in a toga of midnight blue adorned with large yellow sunflowers, winding it loosely around his body and casting it gracefully over his left shoulder, leaving the right shoulder bare. On his left hip he buckled his father's tasseled sword. 'Juguda,' I said, 'you look like a gallant warrior. Go forth to meet your fortune and your fate.'

I said a prayer that he would not fall for some pretty little nitwit. Sometimes prayers are answered too well. A week later I asked him if he had found Her. 'I have, Father. She is Jabu, daughter of Buba of Goat River. I have planted my stake at her door.'

My heart sank. Jabu . . . Solid? Yes, as a log. Intelligent? Yes, as a stone. Well, she was his own choice, so I praised her. A week or two later I mentioned Jabu. How was she? A look of disgust crossed his face. 'That one? I heard that Yaya, son of Gogara, paid her attention and she responded. I have pulled up my stake.'

I sympathised and said no more till Christmas time. 'Have you found Her yet?' I asked.

His face lit up. 'I have. She is Desa, daughter of Danboi of Timlomi. She is small, but she is beautiful and good.'

Fine. I took occasion to call on Danboi, who lived up in the rocks. I saw a stake planted near his door. As we talked, a pretty little maid of about ten passed in, with a pot of water on her head. 'Is that your daughter?' I asked.

'Yes, that is Desa. Your boy Juguda wishes to marry her. I have not refused.'

My poor Jug! On the rebound from the too, too solid Jabu, he had fallen for this innocent of ten! 'She is rather young,' I ventured. 'Has she agreed to marry Juguda?'

'We haven't told her yet. Juguda asked us not to. But in four years she will be ready.'

Very good. Christmas came and passed and I asked Juguda, 'How is Desa?'

'Oh, Father, her mother told her I wanted to marry her, and now when I climb up the rocks to view her from afar, she screams and runs away.'

Poor Desa! Poor Jug! As I said, he was the rugged James Cagney type. Came Easter, and he came to me in great fettle. 'I have found her,' he cried.

'Found who?'

'The one I love.'

'What's her name?'

'I forget her name, but she has red skin.'

I rode around that way by accident and saw her. She had 'red' skin indeed, the colour of copper. Her name was Fanta. She was a handsome girl of fourteen and, her mother said, willing to marry Juguda. Fine! In due course both families came together to arrange the formal engagement. African etiquette forbids the man to propose, so Juguda had proposed through his uncle and Mike Dan. The husband pays the dowry. Juguda and his family had agreed to work for fourteen days on Fanta's family farm; to pay four goats, a roll of cloth and ten sleeping mats. The contract was sanctified by a few pots of beer.

The Pangs of Love

The corn was head high when Juguda was down and out again.

'What's the matter?'

'Fanta, Father. She doesn't love me any more.'

'How do you know?'

'I know it, Father. She passes me by as if I were a dog or a tree.'

'Used she smile at you before?'

'Yes. She used to greet me with her eyes. Even in church she'd look up when I looked at her. Now she loves some other boy. But I don't care.'

Poor Jug, ignorant of women's wiles! He had engaged in that delicious parley of the eyes, as I did in my day, where every glance rings loud as thunder on the heart. Now that Fanta had veiled her eyes, his heart was broken. To cheer him up I began to tease him that night when the boys sat around my feet. 'Boys,' I asked, 'does Fanta love Juguda?'

A chorus, 'Yes, with all her heart.'

'Why then is Juguda sad?'

'Love has burst his heart,' said Iya.

Juguda growled in a fierce undertone, 'Iya, wait till I get you outside!'

'What does a man say when he is in love?'

'He says when the drums beat for the dance his heart is fit to burst.'

'He says Fanta's eyes are bright as the moon.'

'He says when she dances she moves like the widow-bird' – a long-tailed bird of graceful flight.

'He says when she sings she is as sweet as the kirrabong.'

Poor Juguda rushed out in high dudgeon. And at last I knew that Africans do fall romantically in love. What a thing is love! How it changes a man! Here I was with a poet on my hands. And to think that this was the man who, when I once asked him what was the loveliest thing in the world, scratched his head and said, 'A pot of beer'.

Heart's Ease

Peace came to the Jug in this way. My steed Nyagonni, which means Rascal, had broken his tether and wandered off. Juguda found him, grasped his mane, swung himself up and started home. When Nyagonni came near his stable he broke into a wild gallop, heading straight for a steep ravine that bordered our compound. Jug had neither saddle not bridle to control him. At the very edge he threw himself off, rolled, and fetched up against a tree. Nyagonni braced his legs and slid to the bottom, unhurt.

The children's screams brought me to the scene. I found the Jug unconscious, and Fanta kneeling beside him, holding his head in her hands. A splash of water revived the hardy Jug. He put his hand to his head and looked stupidly at the blood. Then he looked up and saw who was holding him and full life rushed back into his eyes. 'Fada', he said to me that night, 'may Allah bless Nyagonni. When I saw Fanta with her hands around my face, and her tears, I knew she loved me. *Mun gode wa Allah*. Thanks be to God.'

'Amen!' I said.

They are happily married now, with two children, Rita and Luka. *Mun gode wa Allah!* It's lovely to love and to be loved!

Death of a Gentleman

Peter, Paul and Pius were my Golden Apples, but Pius was the 'goldingest' of them. He was the son of Gongwori, the village priest and my friend, who used to sacrifice a white cock on behalf of his people. Pius took after his mother Gogo, who was tall and light-skinned – a touch of Arab in him, I thought. He was clever, sensitive and polite. A perfect gentleman, and it was this that killed him in the end. He took the name Pius because he liked the picture of Pius X and 'because he gave us Communion every day'.

In a short time he had learned all we could teach him in Mapeo. I sent him on to the English school in Yola. Then, as he said that he wished to be a priest, I sent him to the Junior Seminary in Jos. From there he wrote back to his comrades: 'My Brothers, I like if all of you become priests of God. But if you try, the world will hate you. Satan hates you now because you do walk with God. One day a man cursed me because I am in the Seminary. I told him, "My friend, I am glad that you abuse me because I try to follow the steps of my Master. I tell you now that no power from the mouth of any man can stop me."'

Pius came home for Christmas holidays. He came to greet me and we talked. Then he went off to help his parents get the corn in. At one o'clock I had lunch, then siesta. At 2.15 I stepped outside to find a boy waiting. 'Fada,' he said, 'a bad snake has bitten Pius. He want Fada to come.'

'When was he bitten?'

'At the middle sun.'

At noon! 'Why you never call me before?'

'Pius say, "If Fada is engaged, I must wait till you finish. First you eat. Then you sleep. So I wait."'

The fools! I grabbed a razor blade and a bottle of permanganate – Connolly's crystals – and ran. When I saw Pius I knew it was too late, his arm was swollen to the shoulder. He was calm as I cut a star over the fang punctures and pushed in the purple crystals. Then we carried him up to the mission and put him to bed in the spare room. Red foam was coming on his lips – it was the kind of snake that curdles the blood. 'Father,' he whispered, 'I am in the mouth of death. Give me confession and the Body of Christ.' I did so, saying as I gave him Communion, 'Receive the Viaticum of the Body of our Lord Jesus

Christ.' After the Last Anointing he said, *'Fada, baabin da ya dame ni yanzu.* There is nothing that troubles me now. I have Jesus. Let me say goodbye to my father and mother.' Gongwori and Gogo were sitting with their backs to the wall. They came to the bed and Pius clasped both their hands, and for the greatness of their love and sorrow, none of them could speak. Then Gogo's grief burst out in a wild keening and she was led outside. The boys came then; one by one they took the hand of their comrade. One would say, 'Pius, may Allah bring you safely home.' Another, 'Pius, may you dismount in peace.' Another, 'Pius, may Allah guard your road.'

'Maria is beautiful'

At dusk I lit the Aladdin lamp. It shone on a picture of Mary of the Immaculate Heart that hung on the wall opposite. Pius fixed his eyes on her while the poison raged deeper into his system. Then, 'Fada', he jerked out, 'Maria – she is beautiful!'

In a little while, 'Fada, she is smiling at me! Truly I love her!' His last words were, 'Fada, will I see her with my eyes?'

'You will.'

'Forever?'

'Forever and ever.'

'Mun gode wa Allah.' Those were his last words: 'We thank God'. He coughed then and the red foam burst from his lips. I read the Great Dismissal as his soul left this world: 'Go forth, O Christian soul, in the name of God the almighty Father who created you, in the name of Jesus Christ, Son of the Living God, who suffered for you, in the name of the Holy Spirit who was poured out upon you . . . May Mary, with all the saints and angels come to meet you and lead you to Paradise. May you see Jesus, your Redeemer, face to face . . .'

That night the drums of death sobbed and throbbed till dawn, crying for the death of Pius Musa, son of Gongwori.

My Red Flowers

Flowers are important. I was planting a bed of zinnias when my boys asked, 'Can you eat them?'

'No. They are for looking at.'

Juguda volunteered, 'I know flowers. They grow in the German Fort every year. Red flowers.'

Flowers? Self-seeding? I saddled up and was off. Only one plant survived, the reason being that the Chamba girls love nosegays, so they bore a hole in the right nostril, stick a flower in and are dressed for the dance. I carried the survivor home and planted it. It flourished. In the wet season its children sprang up in hundreds, each one a burning bush of red-purple blooms. I found that they were called amaranths – Tennyson's Lotus Eaters desired to be 'prop't on beds of amaranth and moly', and they are not absent from *The Hound of Heaven*. When I planted them out in flaming circles and triangles, edged by whitewashed stones – ah, they were beautiful!

Henceforth, when I visited other men's missions, I used to give them some amaranth seeds to sow. Everywhere they made a blaze of beauty. My comrades called them 'Mal's Red Weeds', just because they sprang up so joyously! Never mind. Can you have a civilised home without flowers?

Around this time a box of spiritual books came to us from an Irish convent. I grabbed *The Imitation of Christ*. On the flyleaf was written: *Ad usum Sister Beata, June 1909*. From its pages a slip of yellowed paper fluttered out on which was written, in a fair, disciplined, nun-like hand, this fragment of a Persian poem:

> *If I had but two loaves of bread,*
> *I would sell one and buy hyacinths,*
> *for they would feed my heart.*

And a heart leaped straight to my heart. What was she like, I wondered? In what garden, among what flowers did she grow? Was she fair and vivacious as daffodils? Or dark and secret as bluebells, acquainted with tears? She is gone, with all her peers, leaving nothing of herself but this slip of paper, which I cherish.

It helped me once. My mother being ill, I went into a Dublin flower shop to buy her something green. The fragrance of a bowl of hyacinths, blue and white, smote my heart like a gong. I stood and gazed, fingering the small coins in my pocket. 'Can I help you, sir?'

'Yes. How much are those hyacinths?'

He named an exorbitant sum, for it was an expensive shop, full of tweedy, assertive ladies. 'Look,' I said, 'did you ever read a Persian poem that goes like this?' – and I quoted the poem.

'I'm afraid not, sir.'

'Please give me a piece of paper and I'll write it down.'

I did so and said, 'Now, if you write these words, artistically, on a scroll, and display it in your beautiful shop, you will sell far more flowers. What I ask you is this: Will you, for this poem, and this small money, sell me those hyacinths?'

He beckoned the manager, who looked at the poem and said, 'But what does it mean?'

'It means,' I said, 'that if you had but two loaves left for food, you would eat one to feed your stomach, and, with the other, buy hyacinths to feed your soul.'

'Oh!' he said. He said it like an Englishman, 'Ow!', making me feel like an outcast. 'There is another piece,' I said brightly, 'that you may prefer.' By Gerard Manley Hopkins. It goes:

A juice rides rich through bluebells, in vine leaves,
And beauty's dearest, veriest vein is tears.

'Ow!', he said again. I did not try to explain its plangent, elusive beauty, for it was plain that, though he sold flowers, he had not a flowerlike soul. He gave me a strange look and snapped to the assistant, 'Give him the hyacinths.'

I brought them to my mother, and told her the story of the slip of paper, the nun's poem and the flower shop, which she relished, being of a like mind. The hyacinths and her laughter made her much better.

Crime and Punishment

In my work for the Chambas I had not forgotten the Komas who dwelt on top of the mountain – free spirits, untouched by white-folk's laws, despising the people of the plains. At the foot of their mountain dwelt Baro, their liaison officer with the rest of the world. With Baro's connivance I climbed up and made friends. They were a bit flighty, dressed, you may say, in their weapons – sword, knife, light battle axe, spear and bow with quiver of arrows. A people not to be trifled with.

Now, in all Mapeo there was only one thief, Gindoleh by name. One day, slanting up the mountain, he met a wandering Koma goat, loosed an arrow, shot it, skinned it, roasted it and had a really good meal.

Next day, at the hottest hour, when the Chambas were resting, a war-party of Komas marched into the village. Without a word they took Gindoleh and brought him up the mountain. There they tied his hands to a high branch so that his toes barely touched the ground. For two nights they held a dance around him singing mocking songs, while the women and children prodded him with sticks. For breakfast they made him drink a purgative of goat's currants mixed with water. On the third day his wife A'issa came to me in tears. Would I save her husband? A'issa was one of those who came to Benediction in the evenings. I consulted Mike Dan. He said let's go to Baro at the butt of the mountain. We went. Baro was truculent. Why should they release an evil man, a thief and a robber? No, let him pay for his crime!

Now I, as a youth, had lost two fine front teeth in a hurling match. They were replaced by two new ones on a plate, which I could push out at will with the tip of my tongue. I pushed them out now at Baro, with a wolfish grin. Horrified, Baro took cover behind a rock. 'Baro,' I said, 'I have Power. Power! But release Gindoleh and no evil will catch you.'

My bluff worked. At sunset Gindoleh crept home to his wife, slimmer, wiser, literally purged of his crime.

That took place long, long ago when I was young. Since then we have a Koma priest, Father Luke Nass by name. But still the Komas are men not to be trifled with.

'Come into Yola'

'Come into Yola. You've been long enough in your bush. All the lads will be in. Two new men have come from Ireland.' Delightful orders from my boss, Monsignor Paddy Dalton of Tipperary. I organised carriers, saddled up and was off. Three odd things befell me on the way.

I slept the first night in a bush rest house, round, thatched, with a doorway but no door. Intending to make a very early start I lay down on my camp bed as I was, in a singlet, khaki slacks and socks. At about three in the morning I woke up. In the light of a full moon I saw a figure crouched in my doorway, his hand on my saddle blanket. Softly lifting the mosquito net, I gave my roar and jumped out. The roar was to frighten the thief and make him turn his back. He fled into the moonlight. I followed. His long gown hindered his running, while I was lightly clad. I brought him down, stood him up. He was a Muslim trader. He called Allah to witness that he thought the rest house was empty and only wanted to sleep. I woke up the carriers and told them to judge him. 'Guilty,' they said. 'No man would sleep in an empty hut when there is a village nearby.'

'Punish him small-small,' I said. They slapped him with the palms of their hands.

'Run,' I said, and he loped off in the moonlight.

I am sorry ever since, sorry I was not like the bishop of the silver candlesticks in *Les Miserables*, merciful, compassionate. But no man is wise when he is young.

Riding towards the Verre Hills in the morning, I saw a cloud above, where no cloud should be, for it was the dry season. It seemed to be in motion and to have a pinkish tint. I rode towards it until midday, when, the sun oppressing me, I tethered the horse in the shade. Where a wild fig tree had fallen across a gully, I broke off some branches to make a couch, and lay down to sleep the heat away.

I woke up to see a movement near my left eye. It was a snake, his little forked tongue flickering in and out, testing the atmosphere. As I watched him, I heard sounds as of large hailstones striking the leaves above my head. When the snake, seeking coolth, burrowed down among the leaves, I came out into the sunlight, to be smitten on the cheek by a large locust. They were dropping in millions around me and setting to work on every green thing. This was the cloud I had seen over the hills in the morning. A locust is like a huge brown grasshopper, its body as thick as my middle finger. In the next village I found the children gathering them, snapping their legs and bringing them home to eat, just like John the Baptist. They are very good to eat, full of protein.

On the Veranda

That night, under a snow-white moon, we had a session on the veranda. These were delightful occasions. The two new men were Fr

Tadhg Cotter from Abbeyfeale, and Fr Andy Hanly from Fethard in Tipperary. As we listened to the news from home we wet our whistles. You may talk about 'Ice-cold in Alex', but for the real thing come down to the equator.

As we talked, I happened to mention that there were ten in our family, six girls and four boys.

'Twelve in ours,' said Bill Power of the County Limerick.

'Twelve in ours too,' said Hugh Garman of Kent.

Fionan Heffernan of Kerry had eight. 'The same in ours,' said Monsignor. Tadhg Cotter had six. Andy Hanly smiled benignly. 'Sorry to out-class you, gentlemen. In my family there are thirteen.'

Not to be beaten, I boasted, 'But we have a priest and a nun in ours.'

'Two nuns and a priest in ours,' said Tadhg.

'The same in ours,' said Monsignor.

'Beat you all,' said Hugh of Kent. 'We have two nuns, a priest and a brother.'

'Hold on!' Fionan cried, 'We have three priests and two nuns in ours.'

Said Bill Power of the Ballahoura Hills, 'What are you all talking about? In my family there are *three* nuns and *three* priests, and one of them a *Jesuit* to boot!'

Andy Hanly smiled benignly again. 'Sorry to have out-classed you again, gentlemen. In my family there are four nuns, two Cistercian monks and one Augustinian priest. Put that in your pipes and smoke it.'

We laughed then, and marvelled that our seven families totalled sixty-nine children, thirty of whom had given themselves to God. We tossed a coin to decide who should train the new men. Tadhg Cotter fell to my lot and Andy Hanly to Gabriel Broder.

Our Irish Army

Looking back on what I have written, I notice that I have been romancing along as if I were the only worthwhile missionary. As a matter of fact, I had 1,485 priest comrades working with me in Africa, along with 240 brothers and 445 lay workers.

And what of Sisters? Surely the rigours of Africa were too much for them? No. In the 1950s there were 2,006 Irish Sisters working alongside us, women dedicated, fearless, much-enduring. I have met them in the arid bush villages of the North, in the dark forests of the South, and in the teeming cities, nursing, teaching, caring for lepers – indeed, our strident feminists could learn from them. They were utterly selfless, utterly Christlike, far more so than we men.

Between men and women then, we had an army of 4,176 Irish missionaries in Africa alone. And what of other mission lands – China, Japan, India and the Pacific Islands? Here we find another army of 2,000 Irish men and women. What then of the English-speaking world, England, the USA, Canada, Australia, South Africa? Here we had about 4,000 Irish priests and 8,000 nuns and brothers. In all, we had an army of 18,000 Pilgrims for Christ. Remember, too, that behind every missionary there was a family.

These figures were compiled by Fr Michael C. Pelly SJ, under the title 'A Statistical Analysis of the Irish Missionary Effort', published in the autumn issue of *Pagan Missions*, at St Columban's, Navan, in 1966.

It was our second Golden Age. In the first, roughly from AD 500 to 900, our ancestors went out in their hundreds to bring back learning and the Faith to a ruined Europe. In return, these Europeans called us the Island of Saints and Scholars.

The first fifty years of this twentieth century saw an explosion of missionary spirit among our own teenagers. They went out in their thousands to the ends of the earth. What fueled this explosion? What were they like, these teenagers?

'Let's do something beautiful'

They were ordinary boys and girls, cycling to school in town or country, poor, and accustomed to sacrifice. Heroism was in the air when we were young, the urge to do the noble deed. Pearse and the Easter Rising were part of the furniture of our minds. The Eucharistic Congress of 1932 brought the world to us. Emmet's dream had almost come true: we had taken our place among the nations of the earth. A visiting journalist described Dublin as 'a city in the state of grace'. John McCormack's singing of the *Panis Angelicus* in the Park rejoiced our hearts. These things made us proud to be Irish and Catholic. And so, when the Holy Spirit whispered in young hearts, 'Let's do something beautiful for God', the answer was Yes!

The phrase comes from Mother Teresa of Calcutta, a handmaid of the Lord. When Malcolm Muggeridge, smitten by her grace, desired to make a film of the life of her Sisters, she cried out, 'Oh yes! Let's do something beautiful for God!' These Irish teenagers felt the same urge. The form it took was 'Let me go to far-off lands for the sake of Christ. That is the highest thing I can do with my life.'

They were echoing the words of the ancient Gaelic sermon, spoken about the year AD 600: 'This is White Martyrdom, when a man renounces all he loves for Christ.' The Spirit of God urged them and Mary called them, for they were children of Rosary homes, whose parents turned to prayer in times of suffering and disaster. They were children of history too. Their ancestors for fifty generations had clung to Christ and the Catholic Faith. They had God in their blood. Throughout the terrible centuries, the ancestors lay down to die on bed or bracken and vanished like raindrops into the earth. But not without passing on what they most prized, the Treasure, the Pearl of great price, for which one person will lay down his life. As Belloc wrote, 'The efforts to destroy the Faith in Ireland have exceeded in violence, perseverance, cruelty, any persecution in any time or place in the world. They failed . . .'

They failed, through the grace of God. And as Patrick came and remoulded the history of Ireland, so our young missionaries went out to remould the history of other lands, inserting Christ into it. When I was a boy, a great part of the world's map was coloured red, depicting the Empire on which the sun never set. Except for their attempt at ethnic cleansing in Ireland, I have always admired the people of England who built up that Empire, 'every man a captain', as Belloc said of the Normans. We Irish, with equal courage, built up an empire of the spirit, equally far-flung and more enduring. The builders were young and brave, and now, at the end of the century, nearly all are dead. Remembering them, my comrades, I think of Omar Khayyam's paeon in praise of wine:

I often wonder what the Vintners buy
One half so precious as the Goods they sell.

I wonder what we Irish could buy, one half so precious as the goods we gave gladly away: Wine of the grapes of God, Wine of the true Vine. By all the ways of sea and land we sent it forth in living amphorae, and whoever drank of it drank eternal life.

It was the ancient spirit of Christian chivalry that moved these youngsters to fare forth for Christ, the same that moved the ancient missionary who wrote: 'For Éire's love I quitted Éire, hard though it was to leave that green-grassed land of Fáal and all the friends I left behind me there. For Christ's sake – though I make no boast of it – have I left the people of the Gael whom I longed to have ever at my hand. For love of Mary and of Mary's Son have I deserted Éire.' That says it all.

In these days not many young people seek the White Martyrdom. The Holy Spirit seems to call them into missionary life at home through the many new movements: the Youth 2000, the Focolars and the Communion and Liberation movements that have come to us from Italy, the Charismatic and the Pro-life groups, the many Prayer Groups and the tried and tested Vincent de Paul and the Legion of Mary. The members of these groups are the young and enthusiastic. May God bless them!

The Dam' Fellow!

There are two kinds of men on our mission, the man who can build you a church, estimating the cost to the last nail, and the man who can't. Useless! But once the church is built he can fill it, for he is a gate-crasher of hearts. Such was our Ali. A priest from Galway, his full name was Aloysius, which the people shortened to Ali, the son-in-law of the Prophet.

We were having a beer on the veranda under the stars and still Ali had not come home. Bishop Dalton was worried. 'The trouble is, some day he won't turn up. We'll find him in the bush with the vultures picking him.'

Charlie O'Reilly chuckled. 'Did you hear about Ali and Moffat?' (Moffat, the District Officer, was a typical John Bull, six feet two, a man not to be trifled with. He had fought with Wyndate's Chindits in Burma.)

'What about Moffat?'

'Well, twice when Ali was stuck in bush with a broken-down motorbike, Moffat found him and brought him home and gave him a bed. One day he burst out to me, 'This Father Ali of yours, I can't make out is he a saint or a clueless clot.'

'Moffat is a decent man,' said the Bishop. 'We can't have chaps like Ali annoying him. He's married now, isn't he?'

'Yes. Brought back a wife last leave.'

'Were all the saints clueless clots?' I asked innocently. 'Mind you, Ali does look a bit like St Francis.'

Charlie snorted. 'The saints are all right until you have to live with them.'

'Have you?'

'I've lived with Ali for a year in Jalingo. But never again!'

'Why?'

'Why? Stubborn, chaotic, impossible to live with. Chop would be on the table when some bod with a suppurating ulcer would appear and Ali would be out to him. He'd have a bunch of little kinats squatting in his room when cookoo would ring the bell for the third time, and do you think Ali would send them off? Not on your life. "Ah, sure it's all God's work!", he'd grin.'

'Suffer the little children,' I murmured.

Charlie flared. 'Do you know I couldn't change my pants without some odd bod gawking in the window or wandering in the door!'

'Well, you can't deny that he's a good singer anyway.'

'Singer? Holy Moses, when I think of it! Those cowboy songs! "Home on the Range", "There's a Bridle Hanging on the Wall". At night too. In bed! Under the mosquito net! "I didn't think you could hear me", he'd say. Oh, I could strangle the fellow!'

A young woman advanced until the lamplight lit her smile and flickered on the beady eye of a chicken she held upside down against her thigh. 'My child Ferdinand sick too much,' she said. 'I beg Fada Ali make he come and bless he quick-quick.'

'Sorry, Veronica. Fada Ali no come yet.'

'I go wait then,' she said.

'Let's go to chop,' the bishop said.

We had nearly finished when Ali appeared, his shirt-tail hanging out over his pants, an antelope fawn cradled against his bony chest. 'I bought in the bush for two shillings,' he said apologetically.

He looked not unlike St Francis, thin and brown as an autumn leaf, an El Greco figure. 'Go into your dinner,' the bishop growled.

As Ali turning away there was a rush of bare feet and three or four chattering boys surrounded him. 'Oh, welcome back, Fada! We hear you done come so we run.'

Veronica's voice brushed them aside. 'Please Fada, my boy Ferdinand . . . Take this chicken . . . Come quick-quick.'

Ali dropped the fawn in my lap and the voices faded away into the night. It was half an hour before Ali came back and sat into his dinner. He had just finished when the headlights of a car swept the front of the hourse, making the trees jump nervously. A door slammed and a large, confident figure strode up to the veranda. It was Moffat. No, he would not take anything. He was in a hurry. But could he have a word with Father Ali?

'Sure,' said Ali and followed him into the night.

'Jove, that's torn it,' said the bishop. 'I wonder what law Ali has contravened now . . .'

We were still wondering when Charlie suddenly cocked his ear. 'My God, what's that?'

From out of the darkness came the sound of Ali singing. Soft and low it was, like a lullaby to a child. Ali seemed to be leaning his elbow on the roof of Moffat's car and singing in at him through the window.

'The dam' fellow's gone mad,' said the bishop.

The singing ceased and the car moved off, its red tail lights diminishing down the hill. Ali drifted back. 'Give me back my fawn now,' he said to me.

'What's going on between you and Moffat?' Charlie demanded.

'Oh, Moffat? A fine man. A fine upright pagan man. He has the grandest little wife – I met her when Moffat picked me up once or twice. A little tender thing, not long weaned, I'd say. Rather jumpy and unhappy. Moffat doesn't take time to understand her. Too busy, out and about all day. And a bit underdeveloped, you know – unimaginative. It's enough for a man to *know* he's loved. But a woman needs to be *told* it over and over in a hundred little ways. I told him catch on to himself. He wants me to go to his place tomorrow. The little one likes me.'

'Is that what brought him up?'

'That's all.'

'But what were you singing about?'

'Well, you know that little song called 'Little Things Mean A Lot'? It goes like this.' He sang:

> *Blow me a kiss as you cross the room,*
> *Say I look nice, when I'm not.*
> *Touch my hair as you pass my chair*
> *Little things mean a lot!*

'There's a truth and beauty in that, eh? That's exactly the kind of thing big Moffat has to learn. I'll teach him, softly softly.' And, taking the fawn, he wandered off into the starry night. He must have trained Moffat well, for the 'little one' settled down and was happy.

A month or two later Moffat called on Ali. 'I'm expecting a visit from a bishop. A *real* bishop, Anglican, not like your RC chaps. I've invited him to lunch and you'll be there too.' Bishop Mort proved to be a charming man. The lunch was a success. A few days later Moffat had a thank-you note from Bishop Mort, addressed, alas, to 'Mr John Murphy, D.O. Numan'. Moffat was furious. He came to Ali. 'Look at this! Murphy! *MURPHY! Me! John Murphy!* There was never a drop of renegade blood in my veins! I'll write back and call him Bishop Snort! He's only a bogus bishop!'

When Ali was about to go home on leave, Veronica came to him with a 'dash' of ten shillings, big money in those days. 'It is five shillings for yourself, Fada, and five shillings to buy gift for your Mama.' How lovely!

When Ali came home he wrote a paeon in my mission magazine that ran: 'Not for a million dollars would I change with any man. Let them offer to make me President of America or King of Arabia, not even then would I change. For I am already, by God's grace, an ambassador for the King of Kings. With St John of the Cross, I can say, 'The heavens are mine, the earth is mine and the nations are mine;

mine are the angels and the Mother of God; all things are mine. God himself is mine, and for me, because Christ is mine and all for me.

And so I sing as I go around my bush:

> *When cares pursue me, I'm never gloomy,*
> *I keep on singin' a song:*
> *Though clouds hang low, I laugh at woe,*
> *And go ro-ro-rolling along.*

'No, no, not even for a million will I change. Let me stay here and finish my song.'

He stayed, and stayed until now. In this year, 2001, he is nearly eighty. He has gone back again. Why? 'Because I want to beat Mal Cullen's record as the only one who stuck it out until he was eighty.'

The dam' fellow! The cheek of him! The shocking pride of him! Ah well! His real name is Fr Pierce O'Mahony from Galway, a real nice chap in spite of everything!

My Comrade

Father Tim Cotter came from Drumtrasna, the Ridge Over Abbeyfeale, the Monastery of Feasting. The Cotters had been around for quite a while. The first of them, Ottar the Viking, came rampaging into Cork harbour about AD 900, intent on pillaging the Monastery of Cloyne. For some reason he stayed, fell in love with a Cork girl and begot a son who was, naturally, called Mac Ottair, son of Ottair. They were a virile crew, spreading and giving their name to no less than eight places in the County Cork: Ballymaccoter, Scartmacotter and so on. In due course the name was anglicised to Cotter.

I taught Tim the Hausa and Fulani languages. In his spare time he beautified my mission, lining all the paths with whitewashed stones and planted trees, the Flame of the Forest, Fran Giapani, Jacaranda and Bougainvillea. In due course he built some village churches, got hold of a rig and sank deep wells. I trained him so well that in time he became my bishop. He had leadership in his blood. Sir James Cotter, a direct ancestor, commanded part of King James' troops at Aughrim in 1690. A son of his sailed away with the Wild Geese to fight with the Irish Brigade in France. Coming home in 1710 to visit his people, he was betrayed, captured and hanged in Cork. Another Sir James disgraced himself by apostatising to save his estate, became a silly baronet, and died.

If I praise Father Tim Cotter here, it is because he was a *duine uasal*, he was my comrade, and he is dead. As Antony said of Brutus:

> His life was gentle, and the elements
> So mixed in him that Nature might stand up
> And say to all the world, 'This was a man!'

A Warm Day

Having graduated to his own mission after a year, he wrote to me asking me to come and help him pick a new site. We would start from Lau on the Benue River, whose chief had promised us horses. The dawn came and we inspected the horses. One was sway-backed. The other had quarters like a donkey in a storm. We thanked him and set out on foot. Our first stop was to be So, a village five hours away. As we were marching south, the east lay to our left. The carriers told us that over there lived the great King of the East in his palace by the Mayo Lope, the Muddy River.

I was curious, rash and impetuous, and the morning was cool. 'Tadhg,' I said, 'we could let the carriers go ahead to So, make a detour to see the King of the East, and then rejoin the carriers.'

Tadhg, being prudent, demurred. 'Aren't you the one who always told me never to separate from your carriers?'

'Just once, Tadhg. We're exploring, remember.'

He yielded, and off we pranced to see the King of the East. We found him. He was nothing to write home about, in spite of his title. We farewelled and headed for So, arriving there, parched, at midday. All we found in So were three empty huts and a sad-eyed leper. No village, no carriers, no water. Only a name: So! The leper said the carriers had passed on and the nearest village was under a line of mountain far to the south.

My comrade did not reproach me. That is the kind of man he was. We marched. The land ahead had been fired that morning. It was still smoking and smouldering, sending dancing heat-waves into the air. We marched in silence. No one knows what they can do, unless they have to do it or die. With the setting sun we reached the mountains, found the village, and a small gravelly stream in which we lay down to let our bodies drink. Never, ever, did we drink unboiled water.

In due course the carriers came. We opened our purse and gave them an abundant feast to make up for their suffering. Each man got his own pot of beer. They were happy. They were Jenjens, a river tribe and tough. Among them was one 'lawyer', a troublemaker. We were having our own cuppa in a round house when in barged the 'lawyer', truculent and full of *walla-walla.*

Reader, if you have ever marched for ten hours in the sun, without water, you will know that your temper is hair-trigger. Before I knew it I had sprung and the 'lawyer' lay on the ground. It was wrong of me. I repent. All I can say is that I committed no theological fault! My act was not an *actus humanus*. But the Jenjens were up like angry bees. We could carry our own so-and-so loads! They were going home.

'Tadhg,' I said, 'you are the innocent one. Go and settle it, whatever the cost. I'll take a walk.'

He did. The conditions the Jenjens laid down were that the man from Yola (me) should get out of their country and never again set foot in it, and that they should get double pay for the rest of the trek. Agreed.

Farewell
The next day was idyllic. We climbed up the mountain, started down the other side and came upon a wood through which poured a mountain stream, tree-shaded, fern-shadowed. The carriers dropped their loads and began to bathe. I stripped off and lay in a rippling, sandy pool. The ripples caressed me. I nuzzled my head in under a silver cascade. I lifted my eyes to the green shade above and drank in the magic stillness. I communed with the living tree-trunks and the wet, sun-dappled stones. A bird darted down, gripped a stone with his little black claws and began picking things from where the water lapped it. And, lying there, I empathised with my children's intuition about the stones that cry. I felt the presence of dryads in the trees and of naiads in the stream. I felt that, if invited, they might come, nearer and nearer through the ferns, until they stood revealed, flower-garlanded. I said nothing to my comrade about my fancies. He was the

acme of common sense. And, to tell the truth, to have such fancies you must be a little mad. Just a little.

Well, to finish my story, in 1962 Tadhg Cotter was consecrated Bishop of Maiduguri, a vast diocese embracing Lake Chad. For twenty-six years he guided it wisely and well. He had the antique Roman virtues of patience, steadfastness and courage. In 1988 he came home to die. Six days before he died, he wrote me his last letter:

> Dear Mal,
>
> My time is running out. There is no more the doctors can do. What I need now is the courage to face the challenge of death. I suppose I should not fear. I have tried to fight the good fight, keep the Faith and do the job God gave me to do. I must try to rejoice that soon I will be dissolved and be with Christ.
>
> Goodbye, Mal. Thanks for the comradeship of fifty years.
>
> Tadhg

Ar dheis láimh Dé go raibh a anam. Though a humble man, he was proud of one little thing. In 1950, when he was home on leave, Abbeyfeale was to meet the Army in the County Football Final. The Army were deemed invincible. The locals begged Tadhg to turn out with them, for he was a splendid footballer. He did. It was a wettish day, the ball was slippery and he could make no hand of it. In the dying seconds, when the Army were leading by two points, a ball came skittering along the grass to Tadhg, forty yards out. Afraid to lift it, he drew on it with the mighty left and crashed it like a cannon ball to the back of the net. From forty yards! Oh, glory!

> *And where's the wealth, I'm wondering*
> *Can buy the cheers that roll,*
> *When the last charge goes thundering*
> *Beneath the twilight goal!*

Bringing Up Donal

When Tadhg Cotter left me for a mission of his own, I was given a new novice to train. Let's call him Donal. Having been gently nurtured, he looked at me and my ways askance. Living alone, I had fallen into my own little ways, letting my beard grow, going by the sun and the seasons and so on. This was abhorrent to Donal – 'The least we can do is be punctual.' He was a punctuality fiend. He made a timetable and hung it on the wall. It began at 5.30 a.m. and led on through Meditation, Mass, Office (half an hour of psalms and Bible readings), then breakfast, followed by language study for him and school for me. Office again at 12.30, followed by Lunch with Spiritual Reading, and then siesta for forty-five minutes. Then football with the boys or gardening for him, while I rode around the villages greeting and getting more boys for school. This brought us to sunset and Angelus bell, followed by evening prayer with the boys. At 7 p.m. we had supper, followed by Elocution. At 10 p.m. *Una in Viam,* meaning One for the Road, a last cigarette, and so to bed.

Well, meekly I delivered myself into his hands, becoming the novice while he became the Novice Master. At 5.30 a.m. I blew, as I said, a blast on the horn to rouse the boys and give them their morning jobs. Coming towards the church I might take a spade from the hands of an awkward boy, just for a minute, to show him how to dig a hole for a tree. The minute would become five and the sun be quite six feet over the horizon when I reached the church. I would see Donal's face glaring at me out of the window. Not a beautiful face, as he was growing a drooping moustache that made him look like a Mexican bandit. 'You're late again!' he would hiss. I am still amazed at my own humility.

For example: Evening Prayer with the boys was at sunset, 6.15. My system was the short Rosary – five Hail Marys only, but with an introduction to each Mystery. Then a short instruction, not to exceed five minutes. Donal would ring the little bell to cut me off, which, if I ignored and went on and on, he would ring furiously on and on.

I rebelled against the Elocution Class. It took place after supper. The book was *Barchester Towers.* Donal stepped out into the dark to see if I was putting enough resonance into my voice. Resonance! I was reading a piece about a horrid clergyman named Mr Crawley when the red spark jumped in my head and I flung the book out into the darkness at Donal. That was the end of Elocution.

Nimrod

I taught him to shoot and to ride a horse, adopting the seat of the Saint Cyr Cavalry School. 'Ride off now', I said 'and greet the people'.

'But what am I to say?'

'Pick up the piccans and say they're lovely.'

'Piccans? Ugh!'

But he became a mighty hunter. Everybody knows vultures. They are like scraggy turkeys with bald heads and necks. Rather horrid looking but very useful. They are the scavengers who gobble up all the filth and carrion. They are almost tame, patrolling the rooftops and lobbing down into backyards.

It was Sunday morning. Donal took the .22 and went out. In a short time I heard a shot, and wondered what game he had found so soon. In two minutes he was back, full of excitement. 'Look! For our Sunday dinner! I've shot a smashing turkey!' And, yes, he held up under my nose a horrid, reeking, unfortunate vulture.

But I really felt sorry for him over the 'Affair of the Tea Cloth'. He had three maiden aunts who adored him. 'Let's make him something beautiful so he may remember us in Africa.'

'Let it be a tea cloth!'

'Embroidered with ladies in crinolines!'

'With big bonnets and baskets of flowers!'

'In dusty pink – and pale green – and lavender . . . and . . . and in heliotrope!'

It was done. He showed it to me, and used it only for Afternoon Tea on Sundays. After three months it disappeared.

'Have you seen my tea cloth?'

'No. Ask the Bingel.'

The Bingel was our rough cook. Donal asked him.

'No, Fada,' said the Bingel, 'I no see 'im.'

'What's that cloth in your hand? Show me!'

Yes, it was the precious tea cloth, black now and greasy, ruined forever. *Sunt lacrimae rerum!* There are tears for things – tears I pretended not to see.

In one thing he surpassed me. That was his rapport with animals, birds and fish. His dog was called Rivets, his orange monkey Bisto, and his blue-gray, red-tailed parrot Cap'n Flint. Flint could imitate every sound, from the 'Left, right' of marching schoolboys to the gurgle of water from bottle to glass. He used imitate the voice of Donal calling Rivets – 'Riv, Riv, Riv!' Rivets would come galloping, ears flapping, only to walk away with a look of infinite disgust when he found it was only Flint fooling him again. The three, parrot, monkey and dog, were great friends. Flint used to waddle laboriously across the sand to climb and perch on a little tree. Rivets would stroll beside him, looking down at him. Then he would deliberately lie across Flint's path, forcing him to make a detour. Flint would put up with it once or twice, then give a screech of anger and nip Rivets sorely in the ear.

Flint and Bisto

One day Flint was waddling across the sand as usual when he saw death: a great hawk was swooping down on him. He gave a scream of terror. Bisto was sitting on the window sill, minding his own business. But in a flash he jumped twelve feet to Flint's side, bounced like a ball with his four paws upward and smote the diving hawk a knock-out blow that sent him off with feathers flying.

But what of the pet fish? Well, I had been away and when I returned I found Donal had a pet fish in a tub of water. He had caught him in the river with the boys. 'His name is Friendly Fish,' said Donal. 'Put your finger in the water and he'll give you a kiss.' I put my finger in. The fish, a chubby little fellow four inches long, waddled over and with his antennae kissed my finger. Ouch! He gave me an electric shock, just like touching a naked wire.

I am afraid, though, there was a touch of the sadist about Donal. One evening he spent an hour planting out a bed of zinnias. Bisto, who was tied up, sat watching him. The job finished, he took Bisto's rope and brought him for a walk. After a while Donal saw a column of soldier ants crossing the path, fierce, coal-black fellows nearly an inch long. He distracted Bisto's attention by pointing up a tree. 'Look up, Bisto.' Then he manoeuvred Bisto's hind legs into the ants. With a clashing of mandibles they swarmed over Bisto, who gave a shriek and a jump and, landing on Donal's neck, clasped his head with his front paws. In a flash the angry soldiers dived inside the collar of his shirt and attacked his tender neck. He threw Bisto off and took off his shirt to remove the ants. Bisto went lolloping away back to the house. In due course Donal arrived. He found Bisto sitting on the newly planted bed of zinnias. He was pulling them up, one by one, sniffing each one delicately, then casting it away with an expression of contumely and contempt. Bisto had his revenge.

After spending twenty years on the mission, Donal came home and is still with us. I tell no more tales about him for fear of reprisals.

Mountains of the Mumuyes

'I think,' said Father Hugh Garman, 'we could chance it.'

We stopped and gazed at the Mountains of the Mumuyes. A green valley invited us into the mysterious heart of the range. A little river, foam-flecked, raced by our feet. Terraced slopes spoke of farms and many people. We knew the Mumuyes. They were fighters. This block of mountains, half the size of an Irish county, was their territory, and it was closed. No white person could enter there except a District Officer with armed police. The Mumuyes were said to have a habit of flicking arrows at strangers. The men wore their hair built up into a cock's comb, while they wore their ears long like waterdogs. This they managed by piercing the lobes and pushing in a piece of stick. This grew larger with the years until the lobe could accommodate a disk two inches in diameter. The women liked to dangle a three-inch nail from the lower lip.

Now, revolving these things inwardly, we sat on our horses and gazed on Mumuye Land. We knew it was closed country. We knew there was a penalty of six months in prison or a heavy fine for entering. The forbidden borders were marked on a map, but we had no map with us. In this jumble of foothills it was hard to know where to draw the line.

'Let's go,' said Hugh.

'OK,' I said. 'I'm only an Irishman. You English own this country. If there is any trouble, let it be upon your head.'

Hidden drums in the hills throbbed the message that strangers were coming. We met them and spoke peaceful things in Fulani language, the lingua franca. They did not flick arrows at us. We shot an antelope as a douceur for the chief. We camped for two nights with them. We moved through valleys and ravines, draws and washes and mesas, until in a place of many villages, where a plashy stream ran down from the hills, we marked a site for a mission. Yakoko was the name of the place, the fatal name.

Henry Bubb

When we got back to Yola and examined the map, we found we had been thirty miles inside closed territory. The DO in charge of the territory was Henry Bubb, a Devon man, an empire builder of the old school, strict and dutiful. He would be bound to take official notice. It was only now, like all sinners, that we began to repent. And it was now that Hugh went down with a bout of malaria. So it fell on me to go and 'explain' to Henry Bubb. I dropped down the Benue River in a canoe, to Henry's HQ in Jalingo. He spent three weeks trekking around his territory, followed by one week in his office to write up reports. A hard life. I found that he already knew. Some Protestant missionaries, angry at our sally into closed country, had lodged a complaint. 'Really I must take notice,' Henry said. 'It was all so public. Camping in there! I'm surprised at Father Garman. I'll hear your case on Thursday.'

I was not happy. Six months in prison or a heavy fine dangled before my eyes. On Thursday morning a policeman placed a long envelope in my hand. I turned inside to open it. 'Oh no, sah,' he said. 'You must open it before my eye.'

I was, illogically, angry and humiliated at this. I went to Henry in a bad mood. He sat behind his desk in his mud-and-thatched office with the dignity of a Jeffries. And, sitting on a mat, looking bewildered, I saw the old Mumuye, Ganko, who had brought us wood and water when we camped in his place.

Preliminaries over, Henry told his interpreter, a Fulani, 'Ask this man did he see this Bature – whiteman – in his village.'

Old Ganko looked up at me and said, *'A'a, mi larai mo sam.'* No, I never saw him. If only I had kept my big mouth shut then!

Here was the star witness collapsed. The result, case dismissed for want of evidence, formalities fulfilled, all justice done, Protestants placated. Which, as I realised too late, was Henry's plan. Ganko had been told to deny seeing me. And like an ass I spoiled it by saying, 'Ganko, did you not see me? Did you not bring me wood and water?'

'Yes. Of course I saw you. Did we not wander the land together?'
'He says he saw me,' I said to Bubb.

He gave me a long, puzzled look and drew a deep breath. 'Case proven,' he said. 'Court imposes a fine of one pound each.'

I could have hugged him. The weight of six months lifted from my heart. That evening, playing football with our schoolboys, I gave a shriek of pure joy and relief. The boy I was chasing fell flat on the ground with terror. I recommend that ploy to Keane and his pards when all seems to be lost! And may God bless Henry Bubb.

Ten years later Mumuye Land was opened. Fr Tim Cotter and Bill Power went in to mark a mission site. They wandered up and down the hills, through canyons, draws and mesas, and at last hit on a good spot where a plashy stream ran down from the hills. They began to mark out a compound. They came on a cairn of stones at one corner, then another, and then another. They asked the locals about them. 'Oh, two whitemen came here long ago. They put these stones here and went away.'

Yes, it was the exact same spot. St Monica's Mission grew there, with church and school and Franciscan Sisters. Hugh Garman was in charge of it from 1960 to 1970. There lived nearby a slightly crazed man, whom Hugh had often helped. One Sunday after Mass, the crazy man came behind Hugh and struck him down with a club. After thirty years, Hugh Garman's work was done.

Gongwori's Grief

Let's go back to Mapeo. Gongwori and his wife Gogo never got over the loss of their son Pius, or Musa, as they still called him. Their one consolation was to think that he was now in heaven with God. What kind of place was heaven, they wanted to know. Was Musa happy there? Had he good friends? Had he good food? Who cooked for him? Did he remember his father and mother? We often sat and talked of these things.

There was more grief in store for Gongwori and Gogo. Their second son, Purri, was bitten by a mad dog. Gongwori applied the native cure: he speared the dog, roasted its liver and gave it to Purri to eat. But it was no cure. Had he told me I would have got him in to Yola for the injections.

A few evenings later I was at my door when Gogo came along from her farm. She had been digging groundnuts. She gave me a handful and sat down on my doorstep for a chat. Gogo was a perfect lady, gentle and refined. It was from her that Pius/Musa had drawn his refinement. After a few minutes she said, 'Till tomorrow, Father', and went home. As she entered her compound her son Purri, now crazy, leaped from a dark hut, stabbed her to the heart and ran howling through the bush, where he died.

Poor Gongwori, bereft of all he loved! After Gogo's burial he had no more reason to live. I tried to comfort him by telling him that Gogo was now in heaven with Musa. As she most certainly was, an innocent pagan woman for whom Jesus died. He told me Gogo used to come to him at night, and sit and talk with him. He was certain of this. All he wanted was to be with her and Musa again. Of his own accord he asked me would I give him the Water of Life, the *Ruwan Rai* that I had given Musa. Could he have it too?

I instructed him, helped him to repent of his sins and gave him the Water of Life and the Bread of Life. He smiled then and said, 'Mona-me, let me die now. I want to be with Musa and Gogo.' He died soon after, and the drums throbbed long and loud and sobbed all night and day for Gongwori. I know that when I come, in my turn, he will cry out, 'Mona-me bari!' as of old. My friend has come!

Farewell Mapeo!
It was time for me to go home on leave. I had spent almost four and a half years in the bush, a long tour. I went and spent six happy months with my people and came back bearing gifts for my Mapeo friends, rosaries, medals, holy pictures and what not.

On my arrival in Yola, Bishop Dalton called me aside. 'We've marked a site for a new mission in Margi country, two hundred miles to the north. I'm sorry, I know you love Mapeo, but I've no one else to send. It's a tough assignment and needs an experienced man. You're the only one able for it.'

I was surprised at how quickly red anger flared up in me. Red, raw anger and rebellion. A few years ago nobody wanted Mapeo. They called it bad names and said it should be abandoned. Now that my heart's blood had gone into making it a little Christendom, they would all love to go there! I walked off without a word, and kept walking for an hour. When I came back I said to my bishop, 'Okay, I'll go.'

I went back to Mapeo to collect my things and say goodbye. I climbed the mountain and sat on a boulder. It was here I used to come on a Sunday afternoon when I was alone. Rolling down boulders for my recreation. No one to talk to. The people hostile. Now the mission compound smiled up at me like a picture, the whitewashed church and school, the straight white paths, the flowers and trees I had planted, the boys charging up and down the football field.

I was alright until Sunday, when a wave of sadness from my people washed over me. I had to look angry to keep back the tears. Their faces yearned towards me. They were my children, old and young. I had toiled and moiled and suffered for them. I baptised them, made them children of God. Between me and every soul here a bond was forged for time and eternity.

I addressed them: '*Jama'ar Allah*, People of God, when I came to you, you were like a dry and thirsty land without water. But the grace of God has fallen on you like rain from heaven, and softened your hearts. You have received Jesus Christ, your God and Redeemer, into your hearts. His Blood has taken away your sins. You are his children. Follow him. Cling to him. Die for him if necessary, like the boys and men of Uganda. I go away, but my heart is always with you.'

A yell came from the back. 'A'a, Fada, do not leave us. You are our father and our mother!'

It was Bujjo, my first friend. I saw Juguda's eyes boring into mine, and Fanta's. My eyes fell on my little ones, all my young-eyed cherubim, Beata and Faustina, Michael and Benjamin and the rest. Bibiana's eyes entreated me – she was the weak one. She had run away with a Muslim pedlar but had returned to grace. The following Sunday she had marched up to the altar wearing a skirt made from a sugar bag of the John Holt Trading Co. Across the bottom was printed, in large blue letters, 'Absolute Purity Guaranteed'! God bless her!

Next morning my carriers swung their loads onto their heads and we were off. My children came with me for a mile out on the plain. There I dismounted and looked at them for the last time. I took their hands and spoke their names, each one, and they were crying and I was comforting them and needing comfort myself. Their last earnest cry as I rode away was, 'May Allah bring you back, Fada!' But Allah never did. A chapter was closed.

Riding off, I wished to God I could build a high wall around my people, to keep Christ in and the world out!

4

INTO A THORNY PLACE

It was January '48 and farewell forever to my beloved Chambas. My heart had beaten there a billion billion times, and something of its influence remains forever. I was bound for Margi Land and the hardest years of my life. My comrade was John Seary, a typical Aussie of the North Queensland outback, tall, rangy, indestructible. He had spent his war as chaplain to the RAF. We sent Mike Dan ahead to set up a shelter of poles and mats for us. We packed our Peugeot pick-up until the springs were down, blessed ourselves and set off. We said our Rosary for a safe journey, as we always did.

On the way, John sang 'Waltzing Matilda' and told stories of Ned Kelly, the bush-ranger. I sang a romantic Australian ballad that ran:

> I rode through the bush in the burning noon,
> Over the hills to my bride.
> The way was rough, the track was long,
> And Bannerman of the Dandanong
> He rode along by my side.

Our way was rough too, but we had packed pickaxes and shovels to dig us out, and a machete to cut branches to put under our wheels in sandy or swampy places.

Our destination was called Kaya, which means Thorns. It was aptly named. The first thing I noticed was that the Margis built their homes thirty to forty yards apart, not honeycomb fashion like the Chambas. 'They fear witches too much,' Mike told us. 'They quarrel too much. They no love their brother. They be bush people proper!'

We had brought two masons. We set about building a three-roomed house of mud block and thatch, seventy feet by twenty. While John concentrated on the language, Mike and I organised the building. Lines of panting men trotted in with stones on their heads for the foundation, for which they were paid 3/6 per cubic yard. Pickaxe men dug the clay pits. Leafy girls brought water from the creek and splashed it down on the clay. Youths and boys danced on the clay to form a sticky mud for making blocks. Three drummers – an essential – speeded on the work. There was a glorious uproar, what with the bellows of the masons, 'Kawo laka' – bring mud, 'Kawo ruwa' – bring water, the roar of the dancers and the boom of the drums. The uproar increased when I found that the stone men were building hollow cubic yards instead of solid. The abuse and counter-abuse flew like hailstones. 'Shegi! Babu! Kariyanka! It was then I won my sobriquet Gilangeru, the Fulani for crocodile. The croc may bask calmly a while in the water, then turn suddenly into a raging fury.

Ruddy Mike!

Mike had been working like a Trojan, organising unruly Margis, doling out payment for this and that, indispensable. Then, one morning, no Mike! Gone! Confusion reigned. John came out to help. All that day of dust and hurly-burly, whenever we paused to wipe the sweat from our eyes, we called him names. And, to crown all, we were out of cigarettes. Gentle Christians, do you know what that meant? In the bush, long ago? The nearest ones were sixty miles away.

Night came and we lay outside on our mats, boiling inwardly. Towards nine we heard a shuffle on the sand, and by starlight saw Mike's figure loom up. He paused ten feet away, outside the danger zone. This was the end for Mike. We tensed our muscles to spring. The earth held its breath. Then, in a silken voice, Mike said, 'I bring cigarettes for Fada.'

Alas for self-respect, justice, pride and such base passions! With whoops like Indians we leaped on Mike, hugged him, kissed him almost. He had done it again, the scallywag! He knew he could slip away on private business, provided he brought us a peace offering at night. Poor whitemen! To Mike we were an open book. We found out later that his private business was to visit the Sarkin Dutse, the King of the Mountain, and ask his niece's hand in marriage.

The walls of our building went up. We had cement enough to make lintels for all the windows bar two. John said, 'Let's fell an iron tree, Mal, and split it.'

The iron tree has black bark and golden flesh as hard as iron. We had an axe with an eight-pound head. John swung it as easily as I might swing a hurley, and the chips flew. Then I took my turn and after ten minutes dropped the axe and vomited. John finished the job. We split the tree with wedges and put up the last two lintels. That was 1948, fifty years ago, and those lintels still stand, impervious to termites or time.

The Miracle?

What happened next is so true that you won't believe it. John put up the rafters of split palm and the purlines of bamboo. We were ready for thatching. We were in a hurry, for the wet season was upon us, and the first tornado could wash away our naked walls. But the only thatching grass grew in a swamp three miles away, owned by a hostile crew whom we called The Baddies. They demanded ten times the just price for a bundle of grass, more than we could afford. 'We have Fada in a hole,' they laughed. 'Let him pay us or let Allah destroy his house.'

The storm clouds rose up and quenched the sun. The thunder roared, the trees bent their heads and the tornado rushed at us with the noise of a thousand drums. Then, glory to God, it divided like curtains on a stage and swept by on either side. Not a drop fell on our building. Next morning every man, woman and child rushed out to plant their corn in the wet earth. All except the Baddies. Not a drop fell on their farm land. Our boys were not slow to tell them, 'There, you see what comes of refusing Fada!'

Next day another tornado drenched the land, but avoided our house and the farms of the Baddies. Still they hardened their hearts and would not budge when we offered them twice the fair price. For fifteen days John and I squatted in a little hut. In that time ten tornadoes rushed by, avoiding our house and the farms of the Baddies. After the third tornado had acted so strangely, it became the talk of the surrounding villages. By the time the seventh had passed by, it was the talk of markets up to forty miles away. After the ninth, a deputation of elders came to parley. 'Hail, Lion, may Allah give you victory!'

A long silence. Then, 'Whiteman, why have you stopped the rain? Everybody's corn is green except ours. You have power. Ask Allah to give us rain or we shall die of hunger.'

'I did not stop the rain. But I think Allah would like you to bring me thatch.'

That evening the tenth tornado ignored both our house and the Baddies' land. It was the end. Next day we saw every man, woman and child come trotting in, laden with lovely long grass. 'It is yours, Whiteman. For nothing. Take it and give us rain.'

The thatchers set to work. The penitent ones helped. In three days the job was done. Nothing remained but to tie down the last long mat that covers the peak of the roof where the thatch meets. Just then the thunder boomed and another tornado roared across the bush. The thatchers jumped down and ran for shelter. All but a Muslim with the ringing name of Danganna. He stayed aloft, mocking the cowards of little faith. 'Don't you know that Allah will keep back the rain till Father's work is done?'

Quite coolly he finished the job. As he tied down the last corner of the mat and slid to the ground an avalanche of water hit the roof. It rained as it had never rained before. The boys inside sang and danced and drummed with delight. Even the Baddies were happy. The tornado had not missed them this time.

That is what happened, call it what you like. You may say I made up the ten tornadoes to equal the ten plagues of Egypt. No, I could have made it nine tornadoes just as easily. But it happened thus.

Mike Falls in Love

'No matter, Fada. I love Buma. I must marry her.' Mike folded his arms and scowled stubbornly. Even his shadow on the sand looked stubborn, except where a little wind played with the tail of his shirt, for Mike liked to let the tail hang out like modern youth. 'But, Mike, you are a Christian and Buma is a pagan, and a mountainy pagan at that.'

'No matter, Fada. Buma say she will go through fire and water for me.'

Right. We know that it's lovely to love and to be loved. Buma was of the Royal Family, being a niece of the Sarkin Dutse, the King of the Mountain, feudal lord of these parts. Arrangements were made, Mike paid dowry, and the King and family brought Buma down for marriage. She was magnificent, six feet tall and straight as a lance from carrying things up and down the mountain. She was dressed in six yards of red and yellow cloth, Mike's gift to her. Into the church then. The mountainy men stood like ebony statues against the back wall. The two Ibo masons were witnesses. 'Mike,' I said, 'bring Buma up to the altar.'

But Buma held onto the door and giggled. *'War le!'* I commanded. Mike pulled her up half way. She breaks away and throws herself across an open window, giggling at the landscape. I don't blame her, for this, to her, is an outlandish way to get married. I come and pull her to my side by force.

'Michael Ndang, do you take Buma here to be your lawful wedded wife?'

'I do,' said Mike.

'Buma, do you take Michael for your man?'

Buma, wriggling and twisting her red and yellow cloth, 'Hee-hee! Hee-hee-hee!'

'Buma, do you love Michael?'

'I do, hee-hee-hee, ho-ho-ho!'

'Buma, will you marry Michael?'

'I will, ha-ha-ha, ohhh, hee-hee-hee.'

Right. Consent was manifested. Mike and Buma became husband and wife till death should them part. The mountainy men adjourned to Mike's compound for a feast.

'Victoria, Get Up!'

In due course Buma was baptised Victoria because she liked the sound of it. She was naughty once or twice, and, being chastised, ran back up the mountain to her mammy. But the air of the mission, and above all the arrival of baby Mary, softened her and bound her biologically to Mike. That's the way. Man and woman don't become a symphony until the arrival of the *tertium quid*, the third entity, the link that binds hearts, the beginning of the Family.

A year or two later Victoria fell ill and apparently died. The women raised the keen and ran in all directions across the plain to tell the world that Buma was dead. Father Larry Lyons of Tynagh, County Galway, the then incumbent, heard it and ran to her house with the

Oil of the Sick. He prayed and anointed her and, on the spur of the moment, said, 'Victoria, *ki tashi*, Victoria, get up.'

She opened her eyes, sat up and began to talk. Two weeks later she took her hoe and went to weed Father's groundhuts in thanksgiving.

While these things were happening, I attacked and conquered the Margi language, translated the prayers and catechism and made hymns. We were off.

Death of My Friend

I should have said that Thorns was thirty miles from an American Protestant mission. These Americans were godly men and women, non-smokers, non-drinkers, utterly sincere and dedicated. Their only fault was their dread of the Catholic Church. Even at thirty miles distance they felt that our presence polluted the air. So they came and planted a mission only two miles from us, as a challenge. They were loud in their condemnation of Catholics. 'Better become a Muslim than a Catholic,' one of their ladies told the people.

I hated the idea of rival religions. It made me sick at heart. Remembering a Gaelic proverb, 'It's the quiet pigling that eats the mash,' I went about my business without ever mentioning them, and in the end gathered in the people. The fact that, through Mike, I was a relation-by-marriage of the Chief of the Mountain, helped a little.

The chief was my true friend. He liked me and I liked him. His name was Simda. He was a manly man, but his end was sad. He lived at Gulak, on top of the mountain range that divided Nigeria and Chad. There had always been cattle-rustling over the border but Chief Simda had nothing to do with it. It was the plainsmen who rustled the cattle. But a young, brash Englishman, an Assistant District Officer, appeared. He sent a posse of policemen up the mountain to bring down the chief, accused him of stealing cattle, insulted him, threatened him with prison and ordered him go back up the mountain and to come back the next week for further investigation.

For a proud chief this was an unbearable humiliation and disgrace. His sons, feeling that he might harm himself, hid his sword and knives. Simda was alone in his hut when they heard a deep groan and rushed in. Too late. He had found a knife, placed the point inside his left collar bone, and driven it down into his heart with blows of a stone. May God give him the light of heaven. He was my friend.

'Come on, Rock!'

In 1948 Ireland won the Triple Crown. The Fathers in Nigeria crowed a little. The English in Nigeria were a little miffed. Down in Iboland near the sea, where the Ibo nation was in the process of becoming Christian, the Holy Ghost Fathers dwelt. They were thick on the ground.

In 1949 Ireland won the Crown again. Those were the days of Jackie Kyle and Karl Mullen. The Fathers may have crowed a little loudly. The English took umbrage. A challenge was issued: Would the padres meet them in a rugby match? Agreed. The English drew their team from the Admin. Officers, Police, PWD miners and so on. The padres were mostly old Blackrock and Rockwell men.

They doffed their white cassocks, donned jerseys and togs and trotted on to the field, led by their bishop, Kevin Whelan. He played out-half. The padres won comfortably, twenty-five points to fifteen. But a deputation of Elders came to the bishop. 'My Lord, we beg you, do not do this thing again. Are you not our bishop? Are you not the Vicar of Christ? We beg you . . .' An old lady put it succinctly: 'My Lord, make you no run around like small-boy in your half-knicker.' In Nigeria, a big man must act as a Big Man. If you are important you must look important. You may not run about in your half-knicker. The bishop never played again.

Possibly the padres crowed a little more after this victory. The English took deep umbrage and demanded a return match. Agreed. This time, unfairly, they drew on the Army in far-off Kaduna, young men newly come to the country. They were determined to win. It was plain this was to be a needle match. Spectators came from afar, including the Governor, Residents, DOs and their ladies. The ball was kicked off.

From the first moment no quarter was given or asked. The padres were on their mettle. Cries of 'Come on, Rock!' rent the air and made their spirits soar and their hackles rise. Like all veterans they were skilful and savage in combat. As a hawk cleaves a flock of sparrows, so they clove the Englishmen. The final whistle found them victors by thirty-three points to ten. It was, you might say, satisfactory.

Harmattán of Death

The danger of writing about oneself is that one tends to portray oneself as a Great Fellow, for we all love ourselves. But if, on reflection, one sees that, once upon a time, one *was* a Great Fellow, why not say so and be done with it?

My standing orders were: Make them love you. But it was hard to make the Margis love you. A baby's teat had opened Chamba hearts to me; it took tragedy and death to open Margi hearts.

After Christmas '49, my comrade, John Seary, had departed to build a mission in Bazza. I was awaiting the arrival of my new curate when a strange woman came from Bornu, fell sick and died. She had a violent headache, vomiting, then neck and body arched back, then delirium and death. She came with the Harmattán, the dust-fog from the desert, which hides the sun, makes the bush look ghastly and the nights bitterly cold. Two days later, two children from the compound where the strange woman died showed the same symptoms and died.

My book said it was cerebrospinal-meningitis. A bug attacks the spinal cord near the brain and eats its way down. It can be caught from infected breath, or from dust. What follows I take from my diary:

> *Jan. 6:* Calls from all sides: 'Fada, my wife . . . . Fada, my son!' Sent word to Medical Officer Yola.

> *Jan. 11:* Praise be to God! Dr Heuston, Dubliner, sent 1000 tablets, M&B 693. To be ground up, administered with water every four hours, day and night, 3 to 4 days.

> *Jan. 12:* Packed coffee, sugar, tinned milk into my blue washbag, saddled up and off to have a look around. Went from village to village, dosing and leaving tablets with instructions. Coming home in dusk, stopped by a man prostrating and throwing dust on his head in an agony of petition. 'My daughter! My little daughter!' Went and dosed a girl of twelve. Slept in Papka's compound. Dined on boiled pumpkin and roast groundnuts, v. good.

Jan. 13: Repetition of yesterday. Crossed river to Izge in Bornu. Six down, three dying, seven dead. Chief demanded I leave him all my tablets for himself and wives! *Shegi!*

Jan. 14: Heading home, 14 miles, in dusk. A miserable Bororo, a nomadic cow Fulani: 'Whiteman, across the river. We are dying!' Roughly I said, 'Am I Allah?' and pushed on. A mile down the path my conscience got at me: 'You have the lives of these people in your pocket.' Dammit! Crossed the river to Bororo camp – a few cattle, cowdung, flies, teepees made of cornstalks from which come cries of delirium. Three dead, four bad, one a girl with the face of a Madonna. Did what I could for them, left tablets, and so back to Papka.

Jan. 16: No use going about. Rallied the people to make an isolation camp of poles and mats. Sent word to the markets, 'Bring in your sick'.

Jan. 20: Ten coming in daily. About 80 in camp, each with an attendant, usually a granny. Most patients are children between 3 and 12. Have lost the immunity received from their mother and not yet acquired their own. A boy goes out minding sheep and goats in the morning, returns at noon, sick and silent; headache, arching back, and next morn is dead. Have trained Mike and a teacher to help with dosing.

Jan. 28: Am learning to nurse. Have learned the Three Tricks: the Tomahawk, the Smack and the Splash.

The Tomahawk prises open the clenched teeth of the delirious ones. The Smack – I learned it thus. Kneeling over a strong youth, delirious, I forced open his teeth and poured in the elixir. Instead of swallowing he sent it in a jet back up into my face. Angered, I gave him a sharp smack on the cheek. Surprised, he opened mouth and eyes, stopped struggling, and swallowed his dose like a good child. The Smack is most useful. The Splash I learned from an old granny. I had opened the teeth of a delirious little girl and poured in her dose. Unable to swallow, she was breathing it into her lungs. The granny suddenly splashed cold water on her bare tummy. Convulsively she swallowed, and lived. Now I keep a boy beside me with a calabash of water.

Feb. 1: All tablets finished. Gave them two rounds of flour in water to keep them quiet. Prayed. In afternoon Dr Howarth arrived from Maiduguri with 10,000 tablets, M&B 693. God sent you, I told him. 120 patients in camp. At nights it looks like the bivouac of an army with all the cooking fires.

Feb. 5: Witches! Piercing shrieks before dawn and the keen for the dead. A little boy had died. His mother screaming that there is a witch in the camp who has killed her son. She began to jump into the air like a salmon and come down on her head, seeking death. Fearful mothers began to clutch their children to them and slip away. Drove them back with a bamboo, threw the dead boy on his mother's back, she strode off wailing.

Feb. 20: Twenty a day coming in. About one in 25 dies, coming too late. Dosing them every four hours is tough. Mike has taken over the night shift, God bless him. Sun is hotting up now. Boils the brain and hastens death.

Feb. 28: Margi men are bastards. A little mother came, carrying a dying boy of five in her arms, and on her back a sick baby. She had walked eleven miles in the sun and no one of all mankind had offered to help her; I carried the boy the short distance to the camp, and his weight made my left arm numb. Yet she had walked 11 miles. The boy died, the baby lived.

Mar. 2: Why are women more human than men? A lovely woman came, she had the CSM and her milk had dried up. She had a baby. I gave her husband 3 pence to buy a bottle of milk from Fulanis nearby. He never came back . . . The baby died, the mother lived. Women will die 100 deaths for their children. Men are hard-hearted. Result of polygamy?

Mar. 6: The hot season is upon us, hastening death. 40 a day coming in. My dog Bran barks at night. Plaintive voices outside, 'Fada! Fada!' A couple of nights ago two Fulani boys carried in their father. Too late, he died. They buried him on the spot. Last night I was wakened by the manic laughter of hyenas. The boys had buried their father in a shallow grave, the ground being hard, and the hyenas had found him. Praying for rain.

Mar. 12: Poor little Kelu! Three years old, a lovely mother, a truculent father. Treated her for 3 days, seemed cured, ready to go home. The father came bellowing that she must go home tonight or die. The sorcerer had said so. The sorcerer divines the future by putting a freshwater crab under an upturned pot. Beside the pot he places a few twigs with meanings. One stands for Life, another Death, another Go, etc. Then he lifts the pot, and whichever twig the crab walks over gives the answer.

Just because he was truculent, I said, 'No, she can go home in the morning.' The mother returned to camp with Kelu. It was dusk. An hour later I heard keening for the dead and ran there. Kelu was dead. Her mother had begun to boil gruel in a pot and was stirring it with a stick. Kelu picked up a twig and began to stir it too. Then she put down the twig, lay down on the ground, and died.

Mar. 17: Rain! Praise God and St Patrick! Wet rain, sweet rain, cooling rain, cleansing rain! Washed down the sky and left it blue and sweet as wet bluebells. It will wash away the sickness.

Mar. 25: The big rush is over.

Mar. 28: To bed with fever. Not bad one. Passion Sunday. Three old men came, squatted on the floor; 'Hail, Whiteman, Lion, Lord of the world. We have come from the Mountain of Sukur. Many have died. Many are dying. Come and help us.'

To Sukur

Sukur! An ancient town near the French border. I had always wanted to go there. But it was closed territory, forbidden . . . Here was my chance. I threw back the mosquito net and sat up. 'If we travel all night will we reach Sukur in the morning?'

'No, Lion, it will take a night and a day.'

'OK. The sun is hot now and I am unwell. When night comes and the moon rises I'll go with you.'

'Allah give you victory, Lion.'

Night fell. I rose and ate some bread and milk with local honey, packed rice, onions, coffee and sugar in my blue bag and set out with Mike. We padded single file through the bush, the old men in front, gripping their spears. Their white heads shone like foggy stars in the moonlight. When the dark arms of a valley reached out to embrace us, I vomited grievously and lay down for an hour. I knew from experience that it was possible to 'walk' a fever out of one, and hoped to do so. Further on, where the valley became a gorge, I dipped head and shoulders into a pool to cool off. High in the gorge a leopard roared and the old men muttered a while. On then until the grey dawn appeared and cocks began to crow. A flood of daffodil light poured over the sky and we were at the end. A mountain wall loomed above us, and the sun, the enemy, was up. I lay down and slept the day away.

'Mary, I baptise you'

At sunset we attacked the mountain wall and scaled it. By grey moonlight we marched along a stony plateau swept by a bleak wind. Around 2 a.m. we came on a few stone huts. The old men, wearing only goatskins, were perished with cold. They called out, and mountainy men came out and made us a great fire of reeds. As we sat and talked, chins on knees, a little girl of seven trotted over to snuggle into the blaze. I smiled at her. To my surprise she smiled back. Most children run away when they first see the horrid, bearded whiteman. She picked up a reed and made me a present of it. I thanked her kindly. Another reed. I thanked her again. Then she set up a hunt for the longest and best reeds she could find, all for me. The mountainy men smiled, and one tapped his forehead and said, '*Ginnajo*' – or, as we would say, *duine le Dhia*. She would be a child forever. 'Bring me water,' I said, 'I have good medicine for her.'

There and then, where the fire of reeds flamed and crackled and the wild wind blew, I poured the water on her little head and said, 'Mary,

I baptise you in the name of the Father, and of the Son, and of the Holy Spirit.' That was long ago and far away. I sometimes think of you, Mary, you up there near the sky in that wasteland, an innocent Christian all alone.

There is little more to tell. My fever was gone. We scrambled down that mountain at dawn and by midday had climbed up to Sukur, where we saved sixty lives and spent Holy Week. I judged Sukur to be at least a thousand years old. To the Margis, the ashes of the fires where they cook and sit and talk are humanised, so to speak, semi-sacred. They heap them up carefully outside the compound. The ashes from the fires of the chief's compound were now a hill where trees grew. How many generations? They kept their little mountain cattle in underground cellars and fed them well to make them fat. When one looked down, the mild eye looked up at one, meek and patient, with no hint of reproach!

I arrived home on Holy Saturday night to find my new curate, Father Con Madden, installed. He was reading on the verandah by the light of a bush lamp. From the darkness I made the drawn-out, threatening moan of the hunting hyena. Fr Con jumped up. To this day he swears that he had drawn a bead on me – with my own rifle – when I laughed and revealed myself. We talked and talked, and on Easter Monday I set out for a break to Jos, 500 miles away.

Lulu of the Tadpoles

On my way to Jos I picked up Mother Berard, FMDM, who was going there on business. Berard was principal of a girls' secondary school at Sugu. She was a Shropshire lass, whose sloe-dark eyes and brown face showed her to be of the Cymru stock, ancient Celtic. I knew that her at-home name was Lulu, for once she had lent me her *Golden Treasury*, and there, in a round, schoolgirl hand, was her name: Lulu Clay, 1936.

Lulu – a soft, cushy, cooing sort of name. Like the cooing of doves! But there was nothing soft about Lulu. Touch her, and she rang like steel. As one Reverend Father found when he came late for morning Mass for her Sisters and schoolgirls. Never, never, never again was he late! Lulu could drop a guineafowl out of the sky with her .22 rifle and kept the convent in meat. Now, driving along the dirt road to Jos, we shortened the road by swapping yarns. She had been a WAAF during the war, and after D-Day she had followed the armies to France, where she drove an ambulance for three years, helping the wounded, the sick and refugees. There she met Catholics and became a Catholic herself, to the annoyance of her family. But Lulu had the kind of mind that, when it grasps a truth, grows around it as a tree grows around a piece of iron, gripping it forever. Jesus Christ was the Way, the Truth and the Life, and that was that. She gripped him tighter by becoming a nun of the Franciscan Missionaries of the Divine Motherhood, the FMDM.

She told me that when she was nine years old she developed a passion for tadpoles. She *had to* have them. It was March, the right season, so, taking her little sister by the hand, she visited all the ponds in her father's farm. At last she found one that was alive with lovely, wriggly, fascinating tadpoles. Climbing down the slippery bank, she filled her jam-jar and climbed back.

'But then,' she said, 'I thought they might like some algae. So down again, and this time I slipped and fell headlong into the water. I was wearing a tweed coat and cap my mother had made me. The dip didn't upset me in the least. I still had my tadpoles. I wrung out my coat and cap, came home and hid my treasure behind the pump in the yard. In, then, to face the music. It was, "Up to bed, you naughty thing! You could have drowned your little sister!" '

'In the morning I came downstairs on wings of song and out to the pump to greet my little ones. They were gone, dead, thrown out on the cobblestones by my elder sister who was fifteen. As much as a child's heart can be broken, mine was broken that day. For years I secretly hated that sister.'

I could well believe it. There was a touch of Maggie Tulliver about Lulu. Passionate. I could imagine her going up to the attic like Maggie and venting her fury by beating the head of her wooden doll against the leg of a bed.

She told me these things on the road to Jos in April 1950. In 1966 the Muslims of the North began to massacre the Christian Ibos who lived amongst them. Lulu had fifteen Ibo girls in her school. They were in mortal danger. The Cameroon border was forty miles away behind the Alantika mountains. She told her girls to pack enough food for a week, cleaned her rifle and led them out by night along a bush path. They rested next day, hidden in a swamp. The day after that they scaled the mountain and the following day came down safely into the Cameroons. There she gave them travel money and her blessing. All the girls reached home safely.

Lulu Clay! With most people we meet, it is just a 'Hi!', friendship and no more. But you have stuck in my heart. You worked with us for over twenty years and loved it. Until one day a command came from your superior in England: 'Wind up your affairs and go immediately to Zambia. You are to take charge of a leper colony there.'

You made no whisper of protest. All you said was, 'Everything that happens is adorable.' That was twenty years ago, and whether you live or not I don't know. But I think of you always as the passionate little girl with the sloe-dark eyes, her heart bleeding for the death of all her little ones.

Surprised by Joy

To us bushmen from Yola side, Jos was heaven: a plateau 4,000 feet high, cool air like wine, the *Pax Hotel* for a cold beer, a cinema, a hospital run by the OLA Sisters – Our Lady of the Apostles – and the ever-welcoming SMA Fathers.

That night I went to a cowboy picture, the real thing – the Good Fella, the Bad Fella, the Horses and the Girl – and the Good Fella won! When he emptied his six-gun into the Bad Fella, a youth behind me cried out, 'Oh, he kill 'im baaad!'

After a few days I dropped into the convent to greet the OLA Sisters. They were laughing over a mishap two of them had suffered the night before. They had gone to a bush mission to treat sick children. The Father gave them a good rest house to sleep in. It had two beds, a window and a door. The window was covered by strong 'diamond wire'. When going to bed, one of them noticed what seemed to be a black cat on the window ledge. When she looked again it was gone. They slept well.

The dawn came. The Father, on his way to the church, heard mewing from the rest house and saw two white figures in their nighties making signs at the window. A thief had stolen their coifs, guimpes and whatnot. With a nail driven through the end of a bamboo, he had hooked their clothes, drawn them to the window and eased them out softly softly.

While we were laughing over this, I thought of my old friend Kathleen, who had joined the OLA Sisters and come to Nigeria.

'Where is she now?' I asked.

'She's in the music room.'

'What? Where? What music room?'

'Here, where else. At the end of the corridor.'

As I came softly towards it I heard the tinkle of a piano, a wistful something from Chopin. I stood at the door a moment, admiring the slim white figure at the piano. I came forward. She stood up. 'Kathleen,' I said. It took her a while to recognise the bearded apparition. Then, 'Kevin! Kevin Cullen!'

If I were writing a soap opera I should say here that we fell into each other's arms. But no; we were mature people. But yes; we did engage in that delicious parley of the eyes! Kathleen still had the dark, silken eyebrows and the truly violet eyes. We talked and talked. She told me all her adventures and I told her mine. Her brother Cyril, with whom I used to swim, was killed fighting in North Africa. And Eva Cullen – what of Eva, my sister, her great friend? As we talked, our glances no longer rang like thunder on the heart. But I drank deep draughts of nectar from her eyes, and my heart, which had been sleeping, came awake.

After three blissful days I rose and returned to my bush, refreshed, renewed, rejuvenated. It was the last time we met. Two years later Kathleen, about to go on leave, got cerebral malaria and died. But we shall meet again, Kathleen; yes, we certainly shall meet again, on the long Day of eternity. It is never too late to be surprised by joy!

A Great Fellow

I came back to find myself a Great Fellow. I had sent a report to the Resident at Yola, about the almost 2,000 saved, and 200 lost. He sent a letter of appreciation – I was equal to any full medical team! And my Margis, the breakthrough into their hearts had come at last. My orders had been, Make them love you. Now they did. It was as Ezekiel had prophesied to the Israelites: 'I will take away your hearts of stone and give you hearts of flesh.' Yes, at last the Margis loved me!

A Fulani man whose son I had saved summed it up: *'Kai, Fada, an Baba amin be Dada amin!'* 'Oh, Father, you are our Father and our Mother!' A lovely compliment! I made a prayer out of it, a First Prayer for Little Children:

> *O God, you are my Daddy and my Mammy.*
> *I love you with all my heart.*
> *I thank you with all my soul.*
> *Help me in all my troubles. Amen.*

When saying it they look up and hold their hands out, palms upward. They join them at the Amen and bow the head.

French Tom

It was about this time that French Tom lit up the value of the Mass for me. French Tom was an old Ibo trader who had settled in Gaidam, a frontier town between Nigeria and Chad. Chad was then French territory and Tom used to go trading there, hence his sobriquet. I used to bring Mass once a month to the couple of dozen Christians in Gaidam. The thing about Tom was that, no matter how many weeks he was absent, or miles he had travelled on his camel, he was always back in time for the monthly Mass.

This Sunday when he rode in, I said, 'Tom, you're a wonderful man, never ever to miss Mass.'

Tom replied in pidgin English; 'Why wondaful, Fada? Na the Mass be God! Even if there be only one Mass in the whole world, man must go dey, even if he must walk on his knee.'

French Tom was only repeating what St Augustine had taught fifteen centuries before. Asked to preach about the Mass, he said, 'I would rather keep silent. For the Mass is God. . . . It is the God-priest, Jesus, offering to God his Father, the God-victim, himself. And with himself he is offering us, whom he won for his father by the hard battle of the Cross.'

Jesus himself said, 'Do this in memory of me.' Never was a command better obeyed. Peter obeyed until he was crucified; Paul until his head was cut off. The Greeks and Romans obeyed it, the Gauls, the Franks and the Germans, the Irish and the Saxons. Century after century, in country after country, continent after continent, that command was obeyed. Now, my comrades and I were obeying it in the last, hidden places on earth, and men like French Tom were staking their lives on it: 'The Mass is God.'

My First Fruits

The farmer rejoices at the first fruits of the farm, the corn, grapes, potatoes and whatnot. The missionary's farm is people's hearts; he or she plants the seed of the Word of God and hopes it will grow. Like the farmer, the missionary watches it sprout, cherishes it, cultivates it until it rises shining in the sun. The sun is God's love. It is time, then, for the harvest. The harvest is baptism, which gathers them into God's family and makes them his children.

We had our exam for baptism. All passed except two, a poor old widow named Ijanada and an obstreperous boy named Wayuda, about whom more anon. Ijanada – her name means 'God-gave-me-her', the words her mother murmured when she was born. She was a simple, leaf-clad pagan woman who had never even seen a dress. She came now and appealed to me: 'Fada, listen! I am old. I am stupid. I cannot learn the *Labarin Allah*, the News of God, like these young ones. Look, Fada! My husband is dead. My children are gone from me. I have nothing. But I want God!' She cried it aloud in her own language, '*Niyu Ayu Iju*'. I want God! God bless her! It was the cry of the simple, unspoilt heart, the desire for God, the hunger for God that is buried deep in every human heart, waiting for release.

Who could refuse her? She was washed in the Water of Life that made her a little child in the lap of God. She ate the Bread of Life that made her one with the One who desired to be one with her. Then so great was her joy that she clapped her hands, gave a little laugh and said, 'I thank God. I can stop eating now. I have God.' God bless her. She moved from 'I have nothing. I want God', to 'I can stop eating now. I have God.' For this the universe was made and all its works and pomps, 'that they may know Thee, the true God, and Jesus Christ whom Thou hast sent'.

Who Loves Me?

He grew up, like the great god Pan, down in the reeds by the river, the River of the Monkeys. Cycling along there one day, I met him and urged him to come to school. He did. His name was Wayuda, short for Wa-ayu-da, meaning, Who-Loves-Me? He told me that when his mother was a girl, she had been forced to marry his father, who already had two wives. These, being jealous, had persecuted the girl-bride. So, when her son was born she called him 'Who-loves-me?' as a memorial of her tears.

Wayuda was clever. Within a couple of weeks he could read. Within a year he knew all the catechism by heart, from 'Who made you?' down to 'What are the Four Last Things?', which, as everybody knows, are Death, Judgement, Hell and Heaven. But he had a fierce temper. When crossed by another boy he picked up the nearest stick or stone and let fly. Therefore, when his classmates were passed for baptism, I told him, 'Wayuda, you must be tested for another six months. He looked at me aghast. Then the wild blood of the Margis rushed to his head and, slamming down his books on the floor, he cried out, 'Would that Allah had killed me before I saw this day.' Then he ran through the bush and back across the River of the Monkeys.

A month later I met him there. 'Wayuda,' I said, 'you may as well come back for a few months and be baptised into Jesus Christ, your God.' He was rebellious, ashamed, and anxious to come back, all at the same time. We sat by the river and sorted things out, and he agreed to come back when the rains were over. They had just begun. That was the last time I saw Wayuda.

The meningitis epidemic usually strikes in the dry season. But this year, in the heart of the wet season, a germ came from nowhere and settled in Wayuda's spinal cord. He felt the wicked pain in his head and his body began to arch backward. He called his younger brother Ijusenni and told him, 'I am dying. Run and tell the Father come with the medicine.'

Ijusenni took his spear and ran off. In a few minutes he came back. The river was in full flood and no man could cross it. They could hear its roar. Wayuda knew he was doomed. Now I had taught all my boys how to baptise a dying infant, for there were many such during the epidemic. Ijusenni told me what happened next. 'Wayuda told me, "Take a calabash and bring me water from the river". I brought it. Wayuda was praying, *"Ya Allahna, naa tuba"* (O my God I am sorry . . .) Then he told me, "Say these words after me: I baptise you . . . in the name of the Father, and of the Son, and of the Holy Spirit." He made me say them many times. Then he said, "Hold the water over my head, and pour it on me as you say the words." I did so. Then Wayuda said, *"Na gode wa Allhna"* (I thank my God.) He did not speak again. We buried him beside the river.'

Wayuda, you were brave, braver than ever I could have been. And you had faith so strong that even in the agony of death you taught your little brother how to baptise you. The River of the Monkeys flows on, and beside it you await the Resurrection. God bless you. You know now Who loves you.

Time to Go

It was 1951, time to go home. I had spent three and a half years in the Margi bush without a break. Hard years, the hardest of my life. It was time to go. I trekked around to the eight outstations I had started, saying goodbye. I said goodbye to Mike Dan and French Tom and Ijanada, whose name was now Philomena, meaning Beloved Lady. I said goodbye to my children – *my* children, for they were mine for eternity. Then in June I boarded a plane in Kano and the same day landed in London.

I found my Augustinian brethren grouped around a new gadget called television, meaning 'Seeing Afar'. They were watching ladies play tennis. It was an international competition, and the heroine seemed to be an Australian lady named Doris Harte. It was, you may say, a sudden change.

Fifteen years were to pass before I saw my people again.

5

THE LOVABLE LIBERTIES

The Lovable Liberties

I came home on leave in 1951 after three and a half years, planning to go back after a few months. But my boss called me to him. 'I want you to stay at home and write the mission magazine. You are the best man for the job. Anyhow, you need a break from Africa.'

I gulped. It was like the kick of a horse to the stomach. All my projects! All my loved ones eagerly waiting for my return! 'Father,' I said, 'I don't want to stay at home. But I have a vow of obedience. If you command me to stay, I stay.'

And stay I did for fifteen years, in John's Lane church in the heart of the Liberties of Dublin. The Liberties were the lands around the monastery of St Thomas, founded by King Henry II on his visit to Dublin, in reparation for the slaying of St Thomas à Becket. They were outside the city walls, and those who lived there were free from the exactions and duties of those who lived within the walls, hence the name. Down went my roots, deeper and deeper, for the people of the Liberties were the most loving and lovable on earth. Always poor, often hungry, often holy, they were always loving and lovable.

We Augustinians had been among them for some time. Since 1209 we had lived where Temple Bar now makes night hideous. When Henry VIII, and then Cromwell, reformed us, we went underground among the poor people, posing as sailors, soldiers, labourers and whatnot. Around 1700 one Colonel Byrne might be seen, sword on hip, swaggering around the Liberties. By night he became Father Edmund Byrne OSA, Prior of St Audeon's Arch under the Elements. He was searching for a safe place to offer Mass. The price on his head was £5, the same as on the head of a wolf. But there were no traitors and there was no surrender. At last he found a disused stable in the ruins of the ancient St John's Hospital, which had also been 'reformed'. He hired it, swept it and whitewashed it – possibly with a dash of Reckitt's Blue! That was the origin of the present church of St John and St Augustine, affectionately known as John's Lane.

I lived there for fifteen years. I loved the people and they loved me, and, as we know, it is lovely to love and lovely to be loved. I knew the saints among them, and touched them with my heart and drank of their spirit. Outwardly they were poor; within they were God's aristocrats. They were suffering saints, suffering in Christ and he in them, fulfilling Pascal's saying: 'Jesus of Nazareth is in agony till the end of the world; we may not sleep during that time.'

I used to write down their words and deeds, as grist for my magazine. They are gone, my friends, drowned in the past. But like bubbles in a well they rise before me, their faces, their voices, their hearts. Like the Four Masters who set out to tell the story of Ireland before all was lost, I bring them back to life here, to show the way we used to be.

Her Preparations Made

Jack Finnegan was a builder's labourer and a bit of a rogue. You had to laugh when you met his blue eyes, dancing with devilment under a shock of red-grey hair. He and his mates were fond of the odd cup of tea, a practice the foreman frowned on. 'We were building this house,' said Jack. 'The roof was on but it had no ceiling yet. 'Twas a cold day so I hung my billycan on a little fire of chips in the fireplace. Well, didn't the foreman spot it. "Now I have you," he said to himself, and stood with his back to the fire, waiting for the sinner to appear. Off I went and got a bit of wire and bent a hook on it. Upstairs with me then, with a plank on my shoulder, moryah! I let down my hook and drew up my billy and had my cuppa in peace. You should have heard that man when he turned and found the billy gone. The language of him!'

Jack lived with his widowed daughter and her children. When he came home in the evening and had his dinner, they all knelt and said the Rosary. I joined them one evening. It was during the Marian Year of 1954 for which Pope Pius XII had composed a special prayer, very long and full of hard words. Well, I was never so embarassed: they all knew it by heart except me, the priest!

Whenever Jack switched on the light, his daughter told me later, he'd bless himself and say, 'May God give us the light of heaven!' In the mornings after breakfast, he'd come out of his room with his cap and coat on. She'd hand him his lunch wrapped in a newspaper. Then Jack would place cap and lunch on a chair and kneel down and say his prayers like a child.

In the end Jack got cancer. Poor Jack. The hospital could do nothing for him, so he came home to die. He said to me one day, 'You know, Father, a man's mind keeps going back . . . I'm not a city man. I was born on the mountain above Bohernabreena. After my father died, there were only the two of us living in the house, me and my mother. Every Saturday night I used to go roving – off to the pub or to a bit of a dance, maybe. She'd polish my boots, iron a clean shirt and lay out my good suit, all ready for Sunday Mass. Then she'd wait up for me with a cup of tea.'

'Well, this particular Saturday night, I knew I'd be back late, so I told her, "Don't wait up for me, Ma. I'll be late." Well and good, I went my way. It was after midnight when I came home. My things were laid out, all neat and tidy. I noticed the light on in my mother's room. "Ma", I said, "didn't I tell you not to wait up for me?"'

'There was no answer. I went in and there I found her, lying on her back in the bed, her two arms stretched out. Her right arm was through the sleeve of the brown habit – you know the old people were always laid out in the brown habit. Her left hand was holding the blessed candle; it had nearly burnt out. And do you know, she had put a basin of water on the chair beside the bed, and held the candle out over it, so that if it fell it wouldn't burn the house down. She was cold and dead. But she had her preparations made. Aye, she had all her preparations made.'

Jack's own hour came, and I was helping him to die. I heard his last confession, gave him his last anointing and his last Communion – food for the journey to heaven. At the very end, when his feet were cold and the family were praying around him, and I had my hand under his head, helping him, he cocked the old roguish eye up at me and whispered, 'Egad, Father, I never thought I'd die with my head in the priest-es hand.'

That was how he said it, 'priest-es hand'. Just as, when I was a boy, we used to talk of 'bird's nest-es', slipping in the helping vowel. God be with you, Jack Finnegan. Your preparations were made. In

Bohernabreena you were born, and in Bohernabreena you await the Resurrection, beside the mother who gave you life twice over.

The Quart of Water

Bill Carbery was a Kilkenny man. He was old, so old that he had fought in the Boer War and the Great War. His body was like a chunk of oak, but the legs were 'bet', as he put it. Since he lived in the top balcony of the flats, he could never come down. His daughter Pat, tall and pale as a candle, looked after him.

I used to bring him Communion. His flat was spick and span. The range and everything that could shine was shining – the old soldier taking care of his kit. He used to tell me stories of his youth, like how they used to catch the landlord's pheasants with peas strung on a thread and tied to a stake in a turnip drill, and how they used to fell the landlord's ash trees at night to make hurleys. Tullaroan had been his team, and of all hurlers, Lowry Meagher was the Prince.

One day I said to him, 'Bill, you have no prayerbook. I'll bring you one, and a few other little books to help you pass the time.' Bill grew embarassed. 'To tell you the truth, Father, I can't read. But I'll tell you what I do do. I drink about a quart of water every night before I go to bed. That wakes me up around two in the morning, and I get out on my knees and say the Rosary and think a bit, then back into bed. That's the best I can do.'

Old soldier, hard man, survivor of many battles, he put me to shame. After fifty generations the spirit of Patrick and Columcille lived on in Bill Carbery.

Chosen Out

Veronica Doyle, mother, had the innocent face of a child. Her husband was sick with his nerves; he also had TB and an ulcer. Her daughter Molly, seventeen, had suffered a breakdown after being sexually assaulted, and her youngest girl, Frances, was in hospital with meningitis.

'You know, Father,' she said, 'I was only six months married when my husband got TB. So I went to Granny Dunne – she was a little woman with white hair and apple cheeks – and told her the bad news. "Veronica" she said, "isn't it well for you." Well, I looked at her, thinking that was an awful hard thing to say to a bride. And then she said, "God has big things in store for you, my girl, and he'll give you the grace to bear them all." So I went to Granny Slevin and told her what Granny Dunne had said. And she said, "She's quite right, Veronica, God is after choosing you out."'

Veronica wiped her eyes. 'Oh, Father, I came from a lovely home. At the beginning of Lent Granny Dunne used to take down the big crucifix and stand it on the kitchen table. And if any of us said something that wasn't nice, she'd point to Jesus and say, "Now, now!" It was the same in the month of May. She'd bring down the statue of Our Lady and the youngest child would crown her with flowers on the first day, and we'd say the Rosary before her every night. We do the same in my own home still. Frances brings in pansies from the garden and crowns our Lady on the first day of May . . .'

Veronica went on to tell me of the time she brought her daughter Molly, the one who had had the nervous breakdown, to Mercer's Hospital for shock treatment. 'At College Green she caught hold of the railings and cried, "I won't go! Leave me alone, Mammy. I won't go!" I spent half an hour pleading with her. It was no use. Then the Blessed Virgin put it into my head to say, "Molly, God is after choosing you out to bear this cross. God wants you to do it for souls. If you don't, you won't be like St Bernadette or Thérèse or any of the saints." She looked at me for a full five minutes. I had my hands glued to the railings on each side of her, for fear she'd run away from me. Then she said, "Mammy, is that truth? Is that truth?" "It's God's truth, pet," I said. And then she came with me as meek as a lamb. Thank God and his Blessed Mother, she's a lot better now.'

I could only think of St Paul: 'With Christ I hang upon the Cross, and yet I am alive, or rather, not I, it is Christ that lives in me.' The next morning I offered Mass with Veronica for her and her family. After it she caught my hand and kissed it. My hand! It is I who should have kissed her feet.

Is It Any Harm?

She was a granny of the Liberties, buxom, blythe and debonair. 'Tell me, Father,' she said, 'is it any harm to be praying always?'

'Any harm? You're a lucky girl to be able to pray at all. How do you do it?'

'Sure I can't help it. It's no credit to me. It's just I can't keep my mind off God, night or day.'

'And what prayers do you say?'

'All kinds. I go to half-seven Mass in John's Lane. Then home to my breakfast. I sing my hymns while I'm tidying the house – you know, Hail Queen of Heaven and Sweet Heart of Jesus and so on. You see, I live by myself, so there's no one to mind. Then I set out to do my bit of shopping, and on the way I'm saying the Rosary of the Five Wounds, and the Litany of the Sacred Heart, and the Litany of Our Lady, and the Litany of the Tears of Mary, according as they come to me. I know them off by heart with the years.'

'You're a blessed woman,' I said.

'Didn't I tell you I can't help it? It's no credit to me. On the way home I drop in for the half-ten Mass. Then home, and I settle down to my devotions. But my married daughters keep coming in and interrupting me – they can't stay away from me. Grand oul' kids they are, though. When they leave, it's back to my prayers again.'

I said, with a smile, 'I suppose you pray in your sleep, too?'

'Troth and I do. I fall asleep saying the Rosary, and I often wake up saying Hail Marys. I dream regularly about Mary – her standing in a field of corn and the sun shining down on her. Is it any harm?'

'No ma'am. It's a blessing from God on you. Say one for me.' 'Faith and I will, and many a one. I do pray specially for priests.'

Bleeding Roots

The tragedy of those days was that whole families were forced to emigrate. There was simply no work. Whose fault it was, I do not know. But the suffering was terrible. It was like transplanting flowers from a shady wood to a dry desert. There were bleeding roots that never stopped bleeding.

In John's Lane church there is a shrine of Mary, Mother of Good Counsel. The mothers of the Liberties loved that picture. They used to run to Mary in their troubles, and, on her feastday, they'd place their written petitions before her. One mother I knew, a soul-friend of Mary, was forced to emigrate to Australia with her family. They were not happy. So she dipped her pen in her tears and poured out her soul to the Mother of Good Counsel, mother to Mother.

Dear Mother of Good Counsel,

I, your loving child Mary E. Sinnott, am writing to you, holy Mother, to ask your loving Son to ask his Father to help me get my family and myself home to Ireland. My children are homesick and so am I, but my husband is terrible homesick. He gets so depressed and often does not talk for days. We are all very unhappy.

Mother, you know I was often hungry in Ireland, but I was never unhappy. We could laugh. We seem to have forgotten how to laugh, holy Mother. You know why I came here. I was worried about my son Michael. He was only seventeen years and I came to mind his soul that God gave me to mind. I don't know if I did right or wrong. I was worried about Michael's soul, but now I am worried about four souls, as this place is not like Ireland. It is terrible.

Mother, Ireland is heaven. In Ireland you cannot go wrong, as God and the Holy Mother are wrapped around you. I never wanted a lovely home; I wanted lovely souls for God. Please, Mother of Good Counsel, help us to get home if it is God's holy will. Please, Mother, I have cried so much. I am crying now. I am all mixed up. Please help me. I have the Novena Book. I know your feastday is April 26 and I will pray the prayers every day. Please, Mother, if it is God's holy will.

Your loving child,
Mary E. Sinnott
Mother

'I never wanted a lovely home, I wanted lovely souls for God...' There is a psalm that says:

O God, hear my cry! Listen to my prayer!
From the ends of the earth I call;
My heart is faint.

St Augustine wrote: 'When anyone cries from the ends of the earth, it is Christ who cries in him. He is the man with a thousand hearts, a thousand voices.' With the Mary Sinnotts of the world, he is still in agony, and with him, they are the world's redeemers.

Was her prayer answered? I do not know, for I was moved to Galway at that time. But I know that her letter must have moved Mary's heart to tears, and all the graces needed must have been poured out on her family.

A Vision?

I have always felt that we could do with more joy in our relations with God. Too much of 'the poor mouth', even with good people: 'Oh, I'll never get to heaven!' Not enough joy in the Lord. Not enough trust in his love nor thanks for his grace.

Therefore, in confession, I used to try to *make* them rejoice. 'Be happy. You have your two feet on the road to heaven.' Or I might say, 'Go home now and dance a jig on the kitchen floor. Let the sky fall down and you don't care. You're right with God.'

So, on Saturday night when this poor man came in and made his innocent confession, I said, 'Thank God and be happy. You're living as God's child and he loves you.'

'Faith then, Father, I wasn't always a good boy! In my early days I done everything.'

'And what changed you?' I asked.

'Well, I'll tell you. I was in bed one night in my room. Was I asleep, or awake, I don't know. But I saw the Mother of God standing there, with Our Lord himself. He turned his back and walked to the door, and he left the print of his feet on the boards as if they were wet. Then his Mother said to me, "Folly them steps. Folly them exactly." I tried the best I could, but I was slipping and staggering this way and that. Then she said, "I'll walk them first, and you folly after me." She did, and I walked them after her with no trouble at all. Now, Father, was I asleep or awake, I don't know. Was it a dream or a vision or what, only God knows. All I know is that that's what changed me.'

True, dream or vision, only God knows. But it was theologically sound. Over the door of the Basilica in Lourdes stand the words: *Per*

Mariam ad Jesum. Through Mary to Jesus. She can lead us no place but to him.

The Blackberry Pickers

One chilly autumn evening I was walking north along a boreen out Tallaght way. A yellow moon was rising behind a thorny hedge to my right, and a red sun sinking behind a thorny hedge to my left. There were no houses then. Out from a gap in the hedge tumbled a little girl, followed by another and another, and then a tiny boy.

'Hello! What are you up to?' I asked.

'Pickin' blackberries, Father,' said the eldest. She was about twelve. She had a can in her hand and wore an old hat on her head. The coat she wore, which belonged to her mother, hung down below her knees. Her shins were scratched from the briars, for she wore no stockings, and her feet were wet from standing in the long grass in the ditches, where the raindrops stay all day. In fact, all their shins were scratched, and all their feet were wet and their little noses were cold.

'Did you get many?' I asked.

She showed me the can. It was nearly full, but there were a lot of hard red ones in it, with bits of rusty stems sticking to them. 'Jimmy put in the red ones,' she said. 'There's a bad crop this year.'

'Tell me, how long did it take you to gather this much?'

'We're out since after school, Father.'

'And how much will you get for these?'

'Two shillings, maybe.'

'And then you can go to the pictures?'

'No, Father. We're putting it in the box to help the priests on the foreign missions.'

They stood around me in a shy little circle. I told them I was a priest home from Africa. They were eager to know about Africa – sunshine every day, lions and tigers and black babies – and we talked until the yellow moon was well above the thorny hedge to the right, and the red sun was burnt to embers on the left. As we talked, I was thinking of what Francis Thompson had written somewhere about children: 'Know you not what it is to be a child? It is to have a spirit yet streaming from the waters of baptism; it is to believe in love, to believe in loveliness, to believe in belief.'

I gave them all the money I had in my pocket for a party for themselves. 'The two shillings you will get for the blackberries, put it in the mission box. Every penny! But this money is for your own party – sweets, buns, lemonade and chocolate – and more chocolate!'

Marching homewards, I communed with all the suffering generations who had kept the Faith behind such thorny hedges, in little fields like these. These children were heirs to so much, to Christ, to Patrick, to a grace and simplicity rare in this sad world. It is thirty years since I met them, little ships still in the safe harbour of home. Now they are in mid-ocean, and may the Lord be with them!

A Coat For Jesus

She came into the 'box' one Saturday night, a little country woman from out Saggart way, and whispered her sad story. She had to go to hospital for an operation on Monday. There wasn't much hope for her, and she was leaving small children behind her. That was her sorrow. There was an aura of gentleness and sadness about her that caught my heart. 'Look,' I said, 'tomorrow morning I'll offer Mass for you and yours.' She thanked me and went her way. Three months later I received this letter:

> Dear Father,
> The grace of God be always with you and yours. You may remember to have offered the Sacrifice of the Mass for my intentions a few months ago, when I told you I was going to hospital. I was two weeks there, and I am sorry to say they could do nothing for me. But I am sure when God sends any one of his children any particular suffering, it is for some special reason of his own, and for our own good and his glory.
> When I came back from hospital, my little boy, Liam, was in the Children's Hospital. The specialist said there was no hope of his recovery. Last Wednesday our blessed Lord called him from all his sufferings in this world to his home in heaven. He was just six years old, the eldest of our children. I am sure he is a

little Saint in heaven, where we trust he will intercede for us all. May God's holy will be done.

Now, amidst all troubles, may God bless and Mary protect you.

Monica Lynch.

After reading her letter I mounted my bike and rode out to see her. I met her husband, a small farmer, thin, very silent, ascetic. As we talked, Monica pointed to a little wooden box under the kitchen table. There was a child's coat in it, and a piece of string tied to it. 'That was Liam's little cart,' she said. 'He used pull it around after him. I had taught him that Jesus is everywhere and he asked me, "Is Jesus in my cart?" "Yes, he is," I said. It was a very cold day, and Liam said, "Then he must be feeling cold. I'll give him my coat to keep him warm." So he took off his coat for Jesus. And there it is. 'Twas then he fell sick. He caught a chill from giving his coat to Jesus.'

There the coat lay, a sign of love, of the child loving his God and desiring to keep him warm! Liam was a boy of six; his God, too, had once been a boy of six and would have appreciated the gesture. Not long after, Monica herself followed Liam to heaven. It was as Jesus had foretold, 'I go before you to prepare a place for you . . . And I will come again and take you with me, so that where I am, you also may be.'

Enough! I have given a few glimpses into the heart of the old Liberties and talked about a few of its saints, just to show the way we used to be. There were thousands more saints. There still are, but they grow old. Were there no naughty boys around then? Thousands, but the grace of the saints balanced them out.

My saints had a number of things in common. They were poor. They suffered. They prayed. They clung to Christ and his Mother as their only helpers. They met them in the daily Mass and Rosary. They suffered with Jesus and Mary. But in their sorrows they had a breast on which to lay their heads and a heart that murmured, 'I am with you.' Their faith was iron. You might say they did not believe; they knew. They knew that Jesus and his Mother and the saints were present, alive and breathing, like people standing at your shoulder, just out of the line of vision.

I myself am a simple Christian. Sinful. A believer. I believe in the forgiveness of sins. Thank God for it. It takes away the sting of death. And I can tell you that one of the things I look forward to is the great reunion with my friends the saints, in heaven. I shall touch them with my heart and drink of their spirit once more – the old Grannies, the Jack Finnegans and Bill Carberys, the Mary Sinnotts and Monica Lynches, and all the little 'God-blesha-Father' children. Yes, what a wonderful reunion it will be when all the saints of the Liberties rise up, singing together!

And what a wonderful thing it is to be a priest! I bless my Aunt Stasia for saying long ago, 'Buff will be the priest.' The sorrows and the love of humanity come to your door. The ugliness and the beauty too, and at times beauty blooms from ugliness. The sweetest sound a priest hears is the harsh sob of a man who, having confessed with infinite pain, hears the healing words of Christ, 'I absolve you'. It is the sob of the little child buried for years under the debris of sin and bitterness, now released into the sunlight.

The beauty of being a priest is that so little depends on yourself. You must be a listener, yes, but it is Christ who does the work. It is he who reconciles and heals the wounds in confession, who consoles the sad heart in Communion and gives the life and love and hope without which we cannot live. Indeed, if people only knew it, the greatest therapy on earth lies in daily Mass and Holy Communion.

The Mission Magazine

But what of the mission magazine I was kept at home to write? It was called simply *Augustinian Mission News*. Its aim was to stimulate vocations and get spiritual and financial aid for our missions. People's favourite page was the Children's Page, children in those days being artless and innocent. My pen-name was Austin, and to me they used to send their pennies and prayers. For example:

Mullinahone NS, Tipperary
'Dear Austin,
We live in the Valley of Slievenamon. We were out picking woodbine and wild roses, and we ran in our bare feet and the

buttercups made our toes all goldy, and Helen got a thorn and a red cow chased me . . .' That was Judy Croke herself.

'Dear Austin,
. . . And Miss Grace is our Teacher. She is lovely but sometimes she gets awful cross and sends one of us out to cut a slat in the hedge.' A sigh from gentle Josephine Fitzgibbon.

'Dear Austin,
I am the Sekaterry. Here are 240 pennies from our mite box. Here is the total of our prayers and Masses for your Missions for one month. We went to Mass 303 times, Holy Communion 277 times, Stations of the Cross 91 times, Our Fathers 156 times and odd Hail Marys about 1,000. God bless your little missions. We pray for them every day.'

So sang mellifluous Margaret Maher. Multiply those prayers more than a hundred times from schools all over Ireland, even from England and Scotland. They were a spiritual powerhouse sending help to the workers in the field.

58 Haddington Road, Dublin
'Dear Austin,
Please allow me to help your foreign Missions by becoming a Promoter. I am fifteen years old and I have been ill for the past year. Please send me a mite box.'

That was Séamas O'Farrell. Later:

'Enclosed please find a cheque for £2-8-0. I am slow in sending it, but you know I am confined to bed and cannot always collect the subs on time. Still I will help the Missions all I can by my prayers and alms.'

Séamas's last letter came from hospital. 'I have been here for six weeks. I'm afraid I won't be able to continue until I return home. Goodbye for now. I hope it won't be long until I am in action again. May God bless you and your work.'

Two weeks later Séamas went home to heaven: 'We miss him terribly,' his mother wrote. 'Our only boy. But we don't begrudge him to heaven. There is an entry in his diary that says: "During the past week I have read the Life of the Little Flower. It moved me deeply. When I had finished it I felt certain I wanted to be a missionary priest, if it is God's will." God bless our son. We cry, Austin, but we are proud . . .'

From Matt Talbot, labourer and saint:

> To the Maynooth Mission to China:
> 'Rev. Father,
> Matt Talbot have done no work for the past 18 months. I have been Sick and given over by Priest and Doctor. I don't think I will work any more. Here is one Pound from me, and ten Shillins from my sister. Matt Talbot.'

From St Leo's, Carlow:

> 'Dear Austin,
> When we first wrote to you we were little First Years in pigtails. Now we are Young Ladies in Leaving Cert. But we have never forgotten our promise to your missions. Here is our Spiritual Bank Account for Lent: Holy Mass 1,398 times, Holy Communion 1,242 times, Rosaries 1,310, Stations of the Cross 1,589 times, Visits 2,188, little sacrifices 1,263.
>
> Now Austin, as we have prayed for you, let you pray for us. Pray that we may do well in our Leaving Cert and Easter Orals. Hannie Byrne, Hon. Sec.'

I certainly will, Hannie Byrne and all the lovely ladies of Leaving Cert. What an avalanche of prayer! More things are wrought by prayer than this world dreams of! Listen: for the fun of it I have totted up how long it would take one person, say a hermit, to say all those prayers. It would take 2,538 hours, or three months, fourteen days and eighteen hours, going non-stop, day and night. Blessed be God! And you!

The Silvery Shape

Pat lives in Galway. His mother told me this:

'Pat made his Confirmation and went to greet all his relations. He came back with a jingle in his pocket and counted out £10 before me. Then he read in *Mission News* that Fr O'Leary needed a small chalice. He said, "Mammy, may I buy him one with my £10?" His brothers laughed at him. "Sure a chalice would cost £100," they said. Pat was very downhearted. I asked him why he was so set on a chalice. "I dunno, Mam," he said. "I love the silvery shape of it when the priest lifts it up." Well, didn't he meet Fr O'Leary and asked him, "Would £10 buy any kind of a little chalice, Father?" "Yes, a little trekking chalice for my Mass kit." And Pat gave him all his Confirmation money!'

Pat, you're a chalice yourself, a lovely silvery shape where God dwells!

A prize letter:

'Dear Austin,

Did you see the picture of us getting the Cup for the Best School in the Feis? It was smashing. We red the *Mission News*, espesly the part about the Girl who loves the Beatles. Thank God we are not craked like her. Miss McGrath, our Teacher, has larinjoices. She can hardly speak. You would pitty her. She gave everybody in the class a present. I got a lovely pail green cardigan and I love it because it is real big and the one I have is getting small and tight. Austin, I would love to know who you are. I think you have fair hair and smiley eyes. Won't you please come to see us soon, please God. We say the Rosary for your missions. Goodbye for now and God bless.

From Kathleen Hilliard, John's Lane School.'

As I have sometimes remarked, it's lovely to love and to be loved! 'Smiley eyes' – I like that!

'I'd go Tingland'

Have I given the impression that all youngsters in those days were angels with angelical thoughts? One cold November evening I came trotting down from the top 'Balcony' of the flats and found three teenage girls huddled on the bottom step.

'Move in there, girls,' I said, and sat down with them.

'What were ye talking about?'

'Fellas, Father,' said one.

'And what about the fellas?'

'Molly here is mad about a fella and she can't get him.'

'I am', said Molly. 'I'll die if I don't get him, and I don't care who knows it.'

'Well,' I said, 'if you're so mad about him, you'll catch him in the end, and he'll marry you, maybe. But after three months you'll be tearing the hair out of each other.'

'Oh, he wouldn't tear my hair out,' said Molly. 'Catch me!'

'Why not? What could you do?'

'I'd go Tingland,' said Molly, grandly.

'But suppose there was a babby?'

'Oh, he could mind the babby. I'd go Tingland.'

Molly could be one of a courting couple I passed by a year or two later. I overheard a conversation piece:

Girl: 'Do you love me?'

Man: 'Naw.'

Girl, a quiver in her voice: 'Well, do – do you *like* me?'

Man: 'Naw.'

Girl, angry: 'Well, you can so-and-so off then, you so-and-so!'

The old, old story: Girl falls in love, man falls in lust. The girl suffers. Always it is the girl who suffers.

The Old Trail

In the Liberties of Dublin I had fifteen years of happiness. Part of my happiness consisted in being at home for the glorious years of Wexford hurling, as when, having conquered Cork, the Wexfordmen carried Christie Ring shoulder high off the field, honouring an honourable foe. So often in Croke Park I sang 'Faith of Our Fathers' in full-throated ease, along with 80,000 other Irish men and women.

But fifteen years was too long to be happy. I began to feel uneasy. Life was too smooth, too comfortable. I began to feel the need of a challenge, of a bit of suffering. I had an urge to strike out once more, as the poet said,

> On the old trail, the out-trail, the long trail
> The Trail that is always new.

I put it to my boss. At first he demurred. The mission magazine would suffer. 'We have no one else like you.'

'I know,' I said, 'there is no one else with my low cunning. But I'm tired of it after fifteen years. You'll find somebody.'

He consented. And so, in 1966, I set out to Nigeria for another stint of twenty-nine years.

6

BACK TO THE BUSH

In 1966, then, I said goodbye to my friends of the Liberties, not without tears on both sides, and returned to Nigeria. I came back because mission life was my natural métier, what I was made for. I got off the plane at Kano and made for the church of the SMA Fathers. It was 5 a.m., still dark, and a cold wind blew in from the desert. I found a poor woman already there, waiting for the church to open. Her name was Magdalena, and all she wore on this cold, cold morning was a cotton wrap. After greeting her I walked around to warm myself.

When I came back I found Magdalena on her knees, her head against the door, her forehead pressed down on the cold cement. She was silent, still as a stone, alone in the dark, adoring God within. Adoring and praying without any words, lost in God. The world was dark and cold but her heart was warm with faith and love. Lord, I said in my heart, teach me to pray like Magdalena. She is poor and ignorant, but she is rich and wise, for the Holy Spirit is her teacher and the Kingdom of Heaven is hers. Lord, I said again, teach me to *be* like Magdalena.

In the Central Hotel that evening I overheard a conversation between a young whiz-kid with his briefcase and BMW, and an elderly teacher. The young man said, 'This Catholic religion, I've given it up. You can't be a Catholic and live. Do you still go to Mass?'

The old man answered, 'My God, man, of course I do! I need my God. I need to touch my God with my heart.'

After a while I went to his table and thanked him. 'The best definition of prayer I ever heard,' I said. 'To touch my God with my heart . . . it implies silence, stillness, yearning, love and intimacy.'

On the head of it we became soul-friends. On this, my first day, I had acquired two bits of wisdom, from Magdalena and from this old teacher.

I came back to a new and independent Nigeria. The days of horse and foot and bicycle were gone. Peugeot pick-ups and motorcycles were in. Where, long ago, we had started catechism classes under a tree, there were now churches of cement block with pan roofs. We had a junior seminary, a teachers' training college, and a first-class secondary school. Where I had been proud to teach children in Hausa, '*Ya ba ta pa* – He gave her a stone', I now heard Chamba boys declaim the quarrel scene from Julius Caesar.

Fine! But I found my Ibos fighting for their lives. They now called their land Biafra, and themselves Biafrans. A word about these Ibos, who stick out like a sore thumb in Africa. They are a forest people of South East Nigeria, evangelised by the Holy Ghost Fathers.

A word about their evangelisers.

The first was Lejeune of France, followed by Shanahan of Ireland. Shanahan, newly arrived in 1902, met Lejeune and describes him thus: 'A massive, red-haired giant, with a flaming red beard that covered half his chest, he was built on Herculean lines. By birth a Norman, the blood of the Vikings ran in his veins. He welcomed me in a voice like thunder. Next day he had me out alongside himself, stoking a fire to burn bricks. The sweat fell off us in cupfuls.'

Two years later, Shanahan was in his bush two hundred miles away, when Lejeune walked in out of the forest. 'I have come to say goodbye, *mes amis*. I am dying of cancer and am ordered home.' 'It was typical of his great heart,' Shanahan continues. 'He had come two hundred miles by canoe and on foot, to say goodbye to his comrades. On our last night on the veranda he said, "Before I say goodbye to you, *mes amis*, let me say goodbye to the Queen of Africa." So saying he stood up and straightened his mighty frame to the full. Then with eyes fixed on the white moon that rode in the sky above us, he began to sing in a full-throated, bass voice to her whom the Scripture calls "Fair as the moon". He sang the *Salve Regina*, the Hail Holy Queen, loveliest of all Mary's hymns, which he had learnt at his Norman mother's knee. When the last notes echoed through the forest he looked down at us with a smile of infinite tenderness and faith. "Goodbye, dear friends. Au revoir au ciel." Next morning he was gone.'

The Ibos

Shanahan himself, a big, full-hearted man, became a legend in his own day. Enough to say that when he died, most of the Ibos, ten million strong, were either Christians or on the way. They were the first to hunger for education, and Shanahan gave it them. In a developing Nigeria they became the clerks in Government offices, post offices – everywhere. Hard workers, they became the carpenters, masons and builders. Above all, they were traders, bringing goods from the ports, even to the far North. They were strong, well built, good looking. If you watched schoolchildren at play, those dashing about full of vigour were Ibo children.

Born organisers, wherever a few of them settled in the Muslims North, they formed a church committee and built a little church. Without any priest, they held their own sunday service, with catechism for the children. When, after the Civil War, the Muslim-dominated Government took over their schools – daylight robbery! – they organised the 'Block Rosary'. Children of each city block, or area of town or village, assembled after supper thrice weekly in someone's yard. Young men of the Legion of Mary led them in the Rosary, singing, and taught them catechism.

It was my joy to bring them Mass whenever I could; joy in the children, fifty or sixty of them, from five years of age upwards, sitting on mats, the light shining in their bright eyes and flashing smiles.

Their Sunday Mass, full of joy and song, went on for an hour and a half. Every man, woman and child sang. They loved the Latin, the *Gloria, Pater Noster* and *Credo*. Tiny tots danced solo dances in the aisles. A new child must be celebrated. The parents, with child, lead a singing, swaying procession of family and friends to the altar, each one bearing gifts – dishes of fruit, suffering chickens, yams, and occasionally a reluctant ram! The priest raises the baby on high, prays God to protect it and lays it on the altar for a moment. Then the women split the air with their shrilling, thrilling yodel of victory.

I remember with sadness my Ibo friend Bernard Mmadu, a trader in spare parts. Bernard was tall and handsome, twenty-four years old, a perfect gentleman. He was President of the Curia of the Legion of Mary. He was standing beside me one day at a needle football match between the Catholic Sacred Heart team and the Muslim Dynamos.

In the first half the Dynamos scored, and scored again, and again! Three-nil at half time! Bernard suddenly mounted his motorcycle and disappeared. 'Hm!' I said to myself, 'Couldn't take the beating!' The whistle blew for the second half. The Sacred Hearts suddenly began to dominate. They scored! Again! Again! And again! Four goals! They were still cheering when Bernard came back. 'Oh, Bernard,' I said, 'you should have stayed. We won. Four to three!' Bernard said, simply, 'I knew the Sacred Heart would not let me down.' He had dashed off to the church at half time and spent the second half in prayer!

When the Muslims began the massacre of Ibos in 1966, Bernard escaped to his homeland. During the war he was captured by Northern soldiers. They tied his hands and feet together and drowned him in the Niger. Bernard, friend, as sure as Christ died on the Cross and rose again, you are with him now.

With all their virtues, the Ibos had one grave fault, pride in themselves and contempt of other tribes. The others, naturally, resented this. The British disliked them because they had been the first to clamour for independence. To make a long story short, the British, about to leave in 1960, set up a Federal Parliament and Civil Service. They left an example of integrity, justice and hard work. Neither Parliament nor example survived. The elected politicians were totally corrupt. All of them.

A group of idealistic young army officers, mostly Ibo, purged some of them. There were coups and counter-coups. In 1966 some elements in the North instigated a hate-campaign against the Ibos. Muslim mobs began to massacre them. Between 20,000 and 30,000 died. The rest fled back home.

Colonel Ojukwu then declared Iboland a separate state called Biafra. Civil War followed and raged for two years. The Holy Ghost Fathers stood by their people, helped them and suffered with them. The Ibos fought well but in the end, out-numbered, out-gunned and hungry, the last of their fighters collapsed.

But, resilient as ever, within ten years they were back again in the North, busily trading. We used to call them the Corkmen of Nigeria.

Two Letters

I may have mentioned that when we settled in Margiland, an American Evangelical Church took umbrage and challenged us by building a mission of their own only two miles away. A godly people, neither smoking nor drinking. Their activity, however, made it necessary for me to build a number of bush chapels quickly. But I had no money. The kitty was empty. I thought of my American friend of Roman days, Fr Marty Gilligan, who came from St Augustine, Florida. Thinking that now he must be a prosperous parish priest, I wrote and told him my problem. His reply came from Hong Kong:

> Dear Mal,
> Do you remember the Mass we offered together in the catacombs of Santa Priscilla, just before we parted? Since then I have been chaplain to the American Navy, where I spent my war. Then head of Vatican Info. Service in Algiers; a member of the Secretariat of State in Rome; of the Apostolic Nunciature in Hong Kong, and Chairge d'Affaire in Nanking. A day before your letter came I had word from Rome that I had been made a Monsignor, with a cheque for 100 dollars to dress accordingly. But here in China I can do without the millinery, so take the cheque and God bless you.

May God bless you, Marty Gilligan! Upon such sacrifices the gods themselves cast incense!

From Peru

Around the same time I had a letter from another old Roman friend, a Spaniard named Fr Enriquez Garcia. He wrote from the land of Chimborazo, Cotopaxi and shining Popocatapetl, from a gorge in the high Andes called Punchana. By his door flows the young Amazon, here called the Rio Maranon, seeking the Atlantic three thousand miles away. He writes in Latin with the courtesy of the old world. I translate:

Praised be Jesus Christ!

Greetings and health to my old friend Padre Mal Cullen, who in the wilderness of Nigeria now resides. . . . I wish to inform you of the missionary journeys by me performed amid the jungles *(inter densissimas silvas)*, while the earth four times completed its course around the sun. In return I wish to hear of the toils so bravely performed by you in the African theatre
. . . .

I have just returned from a journey of many weeks along the Rio Tigre and its tributaries, to the great spiritual benefit of the sheep entrusted to me by my good Lord. I also explored the Rio Chambira and Pintoyacu, and sent my report to my Superior at Iquitos. As a result he has appointed two Fathers to be *Missionarii Ambulantes* (Walking Missionaries) with this counsel: that they exclusively devote themselves to the River Indians by constant visitation and instruction.

I myself, with P. Martinez, am perspiring to build a new town on the bank of the Rio Maranon. We are happy to have a fountain generative of electric light *(fontem genetricis lucis electricae* – a generator). The Rio Maranon is an unhappy river. Under its waters dwell shoals of most savage fish called Piranhas. Being endowed with teeth like concave razors, should a man fall among them his flesh would totally depart from his bones in three minutes. An American friend of mine dangled his hand in the water, his finger being slightly wounded, whereat the Piranha, smelling, approached and swiftly tore it from his hand. The alligator sleeps in this river, while on its banks the boa constrictor waits, to the detriment of the indigenous peoples.

I have returned from a holiday in Iquitos, where I listened to a concert whose exquisite music gave delectation to the ears of many. I, too, gave an allocution concerning my journeys, over the radio-phonic waves *(per undas radiophonicas)*. . . .

My dearest friend, I beg you to write me of the adventures performed by you in the African theatre. I am your most devoted friend,

P. Enriquez Garcia OSA

God bless Enriquez, and Marty, and me, and all who fared forth for Christ since the days of Peter and Paul.

'I shall be happy'

In Africa, water is life. It is scarce and precious. When you come home to Ireland you are amazed to see people wasting water. I was therefore happy when Angelino Monaco sank a borehole for me. It was a grace and a blessing.

Angelino worked with an English company. Every weekend he beered away the week's sun and sand, alone in his shack. Sunday nights he rolled up to me. 'You are *simpatico*, Padre. Not cold like the English. With you I can reflect on life. I am a lonely man, Padre. So lonely! It is – how you say? – the afternoon of my life, and nobody loves me. No bambino to call me Papa.'

He was at the sentimental stage. A tear trickled down his nose and threatened his beer. I did not begrudge him his reflections. They were an escape from a rugged, lonely life – his music, his grand opera. 'The trouble with you, Angelino,' I said, 'is that you are a godless man. It is a pity you are not a Catholic.'

The hands flew out and the brown eyes expressed shock. 'Padre! Padre mio! How can you say such things? What am I then? A Protestante? But naturally I am a Catholic – vero, Romano, Apostolico! Did I not come to Mass for Christmas? And the Mission, have I not help you in many ways? Scaffolding, labourers, cement mixer, one beautiful well? Padre, you hurt my heart!'

'I am grateful for your help, Angelino. But you might come to Mass on Sundays to worship your God.'

'Ah, Padre, you must know I am a man of affairs. All my life I have work – oh, so hard. And fight! As a boy for Mussolini in Abyssinia. As a man with Rommel in the desert. Look at my wound.'

He bared his great hairy chest to show where a bullet had sliced across it. 'So many fights! So many works! So many worries. But some day, Padre, I shall be happy. Some day I shall retire. Back to my beloved Genazzano. There I shall learn all the things I never had time to when a boy. About the Padre Eterno and the Madonna most beautiful. You shall see me, Padre, an old man, very quiet, in my beloved town. My hair is white. I am serene. I kneel before the

Madonna, the Madre del Buon' Consiglio. I raise to her my eyes, my eyes of sin. I say, "*Sancta Maria, ora pro me, peccatore, nune, et in hora mortis.* Amen'".

He crossed his hands on his chest and his eyes filled with tears. He wept at the picture of the evening of his life.

'But tonight, Padre, I am lonely. No *bambino* to call me Papa!'

'Why didn't you ever marry, Angelino? Did you never fall in love?'

'In love? *L'amore*? Padre mio, I am never out of love. It is the fault of my heart. It is – how you say? – too susceptible. Every pretty girl I see, I am in love. I walk down a street and before I reach the end I am in love! A young girl raises her arms in song, and presto! I am in love. To me the eyes of every young girl are – how you say? – waters, pools of Paradise.'

He leant forward and tapped my knee. 'Padre, every man is a leetle mad. Just a leetle. Some smell madness hidden inside, eh? With me it is to love one hundred girls all together. If I could marry one hundred girls – *bene!* But when all are so good and beautiful, how can I choose? Suppose I should make an error of judgement? Eh? And so I remain Platonic. That is the tragedy of the heart of Angelino Monaco. It is a Platonic heart. It loves from far away and remains forever lonely.'

The teardrop threatened his beer again. 'Far from Plato you were reared!' I said. 'You'll end up by marrying a rich fat widow.'

When the rains came he went home to Italy on leave. After three months I had a cable: would I kindly meet him at the airstrip. I saw the Dove come dropping down out of the harmattan, saw Monaco appear and turn back to help out a slender figure in white. 'Crikey!' I said aloud, 'He's gone and done it!'

'Meet my wife Rosina, Padre,' he beamed.

It wasn't that she was lovely, golden, fresh as an April morning. It was her smile. Like the smiles of all good children, the raw materials, so to speak, were but certain curvings of the lips, the cheeks, and a gleam of the soul as through crystal. But, looking into her blue eyes as she smiled, I could only remember his own words, 'pool of Paradise'.

I drove them over to a shack in the camp. The shack was a two-roomed affair with rusty tins lying about. Rosina had no word of English except 'Pleas' and 'tank you'. Monaco's boys were there to meet him, two red-fezzed Kanuri Muslims, their tribal marks scored deep in their cheeks like gridirons. Rosina started back as if they were goblins and caught Monaco's hand. He lifted her over the threshold like a straw and laughed, 'We shall make this place into a palazzo for you, carina.'

I drove away wondering. She could not be more than seventeen. Suppose I should make an error of judgement? He had said that once. I wondered.

The Way of Love

The next morning he dropped over to tell me all about it. He embraced me. 'Ah, Padre, you behold a new man. Angelino Monaco is born again. Ah, my Rosina – such innocence! Such a leetle, leetle child! I am – how you say? – in state of grace. I am happiness. It is the power of love. Padre, I am not worthy.'

'Well then, I hope you will bring her to Mass on Sundays.'

'Padre, every morning, every night, I kneel and pray beside my leetle Madonna. I am a new-born child again.'

Then, like Gigli singing grand opera, he told me the story of his love. Blow by blow he revealed how his heart had ceased to be Platonic. And I, knowing every blade of grass in Genazzano since my student days, saw the idyll unfold before my eyes.

He had gone for a stroll out under the castle archway and up the road past San Pio. The peasants noted how the sun blazed on his immaculate white suit and remarked, 'There goes a man of substance, a man of leisure. He has no need to labour like us.' He came to a country inn, white walls and red tiles nestling under a chestnut tree. A vine-covered pergola shadowed its door. A rustic seat invited him. He ordered a bottle of Frascati – you know, Padre, that noble wine with the long, lingering bouquet. He sipped. He gazed kindly on a little wayside shrine of the Madonna across the road. He gazed across the valley to the opposite hillside. People were working over there, passing from sunlight to shadow under the silver-grey olive groves. The bees were going on their little journeys above his head; the cicadas sang in the sunlit branches. Africa fell away. He was at peace.

The singing of girls woke him up, the wild sweet singing of the hills. The girls were coming down from the vineyards, each with a bundle of firewood on her kerchiefed head, and they sang of love. They sang:

> *Fiorin' fiorello,*
> *L' amor' e bello*
> *Vicin' a te.*

They stopped and burst into laughter when they saw the stranger. One of them was slender and golden. As they passed on, she threw a flower at the feet of the Madonna, as is the custom of girls who are praying for a good husband. It was she who picked up the thread of a new song, one of the old hill songs that sang of the sadness of love, plaintive as the sigh of a broken heart:

> *Non si fa piu l'amor con te, carina!*

Never again shall we make love, my dearest! Angelino stood peering through the vine leaves. His heart had flown from his bosom in the old, Platonic way, and nestled in her hand.

On the following evening he sat there fully awake. The girls came down singing and again broke off in pretty confusion when they saw the stranger. Again it was the golden one who threw the flower to the Madonna and picked up the thread of song:

> *I journeyed to Rome to pray in Saint Peter's*
> *But when I came to the colonnade,*
> *A thought of you came to me, and I turned back.*

Angelino put his hand to his heart. It was burning. On the third evening the message of the song was this:

> *And when you pass our house at night, then sing,*
> *And I, who am in bed, will hear you,*
> *And turn my back on my mother, and weep, weep.*

On the fourth evening the song remarked plaintively:

> *And when you came to me at evening,*
> *The best chair was kept for you.*

I have given it away now,
Because you come no more.

It was enough. Fate had chosen for Angelino. Plato was vanquished.

He visited her home. He visited over and over. The best chair was kept for him. He opened his mind to her parents and they consented. Rosina was young, very young. But then, Angelino was a man of substance. And they were so poor. Rosina would never know hunger or unkindness. They consented, but Rosina must decide for herself.

When the moon rode high, he walked her up to the shrine of the Madonna. He was older, yes, he admitted, but his heart was young. Together they would fly away through the blue sky to Africa. Rosina would never again sully her hands with work.

'But – Africa,' she murmured timidly, 'Uncle Armando – he was a soldier – he said to me, Africa is ugly. So much sand. So many flies. So very lonely.'

'Lonely?' he echoed. 'Oh, so lonely! So often I have gazed up at this same moon and my heart has longed and longed for what I knew not. But now I know. It longed for love.'

She raised her eyes. The hills were swimming in moonlight. She saw the strings of light, like beads, that marked other little hill towns. She heard the muted cries of children at play down in Genazzano. 'I am afraid,' she said. 'I am only a little girl. To leave my papa and my mamma, my friends, my little town . . . Africa is so far away.'

'Ah, carina,' he crooned, 'with me you shall never be afraid. With me you shall never be lonely. The roses of life shall be yours, the thorns I shall keep for myself.'

She nestled towards him. Slowly, like a sigh, she named his name for the first time. 'Angelino . . . it is true. You are as good as a piece of bread.'

That was the story. I saw the olives, the vines, the glory of the moon. I saw the new man before me. And I had misgivings. 'Angelino,' I said, 'you have taken a little flower of Genazzano and brought it out to this – Africa. Take care. Take very good care it does not wither.'

He struck his great chest and laughed. 'Have no fear, Padre. My love – it is supreme. It can conquer all things.'

The Withering Rose

The trouble started when Monaco changed from day to night shift. The well head was a mile away from his shack. One night I heard banging and sobbing at my door. Rosina had panicked and ran all the way to the mission. Madre mia, those terrible black people, the snakes, the fearful noises of the night. I sent for Monaco. He gathered her in his great arms, crooning over her like a mother, and carried her home. Two nights later she panicked again.

At this stage I went on a tour of my out-stations and was absent for two weeks. I came back to find a changed Monaco. Always, while he faced life alone, he had a little joke in reserve, a little irony. A laugh at life. Now his shield was gone. The brown eyes were confused and suffering. 'Padre, tell me what to do. It is Rosina. She cannot sleep. She cannot stay alone. She will go mad.'

'I can think of only one thing,' I said. 'Rig her up a bed and a mosquito net in the back of the lorry and let her sleep near the well when you're on night shift.' He tried it. Rosina tried to sleep under the glare of the lamps, beside the rattle of machinery and the grunting of the crew. At the end of the week she was a ghost of herself. She had ceased to smile.

Monaco tried one last gamble. He had himself posted to a project out in the bush where there was only day work. I don't know what happened out there. I do know that the Bornu bush country can be deadly. On endless sandy plains clumps of camel-thorn grow. There is nothing else. And when in the dry season the Sahara wind blows up the sand fog that hangs in the sky for months, the land is ghastly and silent as death. When he brought in Rosina she had ceased to talk. Her eyes were empty. Quietly, without complaining, her mind seemed to have died.

The doctor said she had amentia something. She must go home on the next plane. I drove them to the airstrip and waited till the Dove came. Monaco carried Rosina in and stepped out to say goodbye to me. He put his arms around me. All he said was '*Ora pro me*', and sobbed and was gone.

I drove home with a lump rising in my throat, hearing his voice through the engine: 'Ah, Padre, all my life I have work, ahh, so hard! And fight! As a boy with Mussolini in Abyssinia. As a man with

Rommel in the desert. So many fights! So many works. So many worries. . . . But some day, Padre, I shall be happy . . . Some day I shall be happy. . .'

Donald Dussek

A thousand people may touch our lives and pass on, unremembered. With two or three we may forge a bond for life. The one I write of here is dead, and has haunted me for fifty years.

Donald Dussek of his Majesty's Colonial Service rode into our mission one day, slim, straight and courteous. As he lifted his helmet in greeting, the sun shone on his fair hair and blue eyes, and I felt my Irish reserve towards Englishmen melt a little. Sir Lancelot, I thought, riding down to Camelot. We invited him to dinner that night. He was twenty-three years old, fresh from Cambridge. He had come to Chambaland to command them to grow more groundnuts to help the war effort. His first act, on setting up his little trekking table, was to place two framed photographs on it. 'My mother and my fiancée,' he smiled.

Donald and I shot a couple of guineas for dinner and got out our good delph. He came at dusk and had hardly seated himself when he enquired, in his charming, deliberate voice, 'What is the attitude of the Catholic Church to Communism? – of course, I am not a Christian.'

He sat back then, with the air of a boy who has put a match to a squib, expecting us bearded, rustic missionaries to register shock. We bore the impact bravely, however, and joined battle. That was all he wanted. Until midnight we argued over everything from the existence of God to Pavlov's dogs.

Science, for him, was God and salvation. Science would one day so condition human reflexes that people would become anti-war, anti-vice and lovers of virtue. He was innocent; delightful to argue with, giving and taking with a laugh. Having read Ancient and Modern History he was well versed in ancient and modern paganism, but ignorant of Christ. Like many moderns he professed admiration for Marcus Aurelius, Confucius and the rest, but was strangely shy of Christ. The rub was, as we pointed out, that one could admire the ancients while remaining uninvolved. But Christ had made the terrific claim that he was God, the Way, the Truth and the Life, and demanded unconditional allegiance.

At midnight we showed him back to the rest house. Since it was full-moon time the jolly Chambas were enjoying a moonlit dance. Dussek was mortified. He strode among the leafy maidens and the booming drums and silenced them with an imperial gesture. 'Have you not had commands? Did I not command you to be in your farms at dawn to plant groundnuts? Away to your beds!' He was innocent, and he spoke Hausa with a nice Cambridge accent.

Once, in Yola, he invited me to his weekly gramophone recital. 'To keep us civilised,' he said. The Resident was there, the DO and the MO with their wives. Johnny O'Hara was not there. Johnny was Liverpool-Irish; a foreman of works who had once been middle-weight boxing champion of the Empire. He had knocked around the Far East for years and had once passed a tiger in a street of Singapore at dawn. He drank a half bottle of whiskey each evening, if he could get it. 'But never before sundown,' he said. 'I have my principles.' He was also our good friend, ready to help and to 'condemn' anything we needed from the government store!

I found that Dussek had spread the fame of our argument around the station. 'And what I liked about you people was that when I said I wasn't a Christian, you didn't see horns sprouting out of my head.' The evening was sweetened by a flagon of wine he had got from over the French border. We were immersed in Beethoven's *Pastorale* when Johnny O'Hara appeared at the door, clad in singlet and sarong. 'Music!' he moaned. 'I hear music!' Then his eye fell on a Mona Lisa that graced Dussek's wall. He staggered over to it and raised his arms appealingly. 'Ah, my wifie. My poor, poor wifie far away.' Then he soared into a heart-breaking rendition of 'Danny Boy'.

Poor Dussek was mortified. Coarse facts of life should stay out of the drawing room. To him, Johnny was a coarse fact. To me he was a friend. I put my arm around him and led him home. Soon after, he was transferred to Maiduguri Station, two hundred miles away, and went down with a bad fever. He asked for a priest. A message was sent to Yola. Monsignor Paddy Dalton set off in the pick-up, carrying a shovel and a machete to cut branches to put under the wheels, for it was the wet season and the dirt track was bad. When he arrived, John

O'Hara was already with his God. May you rest in peace, old friend.

The war was over when I next met Dussek. I rode into a bush rest house to find a wan and wasted Dussek sitting there. Gone was Sir Lancelot. Gone was the laughing unbeliever who liked to startle Christians. 'Ah, Father,' he said wistfully, 'it's a long time since we had an argument.'

Things had gone wrong for him. He was suffering from endless stomach trouble. I wondered. I knew there were many subtle ways of administering poison. His mother had died and his fiancée had tired of waiting for her Empire-builder. His work? Disillusioned. Believing eagerly in justice, he was shocked to discover that the Paramount Chief was guilty of slave trafficking and other bad things. Dussek set about gathering evidence to bring him to book. His superior officers merely filed the evidence. Dussek persisted. Finally he was told, 'Look, we know what's going on. But get rid of one rascal and another pops up. Better let sleeping dogs lie.'

He was a man deeply hurt, deeply sad and in need of healing. 'What I envy about you people,' he said, 'is your absolute certainty. A God who is love. One who became man and died for the human race. The idea attracts me. If only it were true! But I fear it is too good to be true . . . But if I were to become anything it would be a Catholic.'

That was my last meeting with Dussek. Next morning I bade him goodbye and rode away jauntily. I have blamed myself ever since. To attend a dying African I would have ridden for days. Here was a man whose spirit was dying, a child crying in the dark, and I was content to talk to him in an airy, detached way, as if faith in Christ were but of speculative importance. I should have stayed with him, urged and pleaded with him. But I didn't. Too damnably polite. I rode off and left him there.

A month later he was invalided home. He joined a publishing company for six months. Then he returned to the land of his birth, to Malaya, where his father had been a District Commissioner. Within the year he got tuberculosis and died.

God be with you, Donal Dussek. We shall meet again. Our God is the God of Allowances.

The Young Lion

I would like to relate all the adventures of these last twenty-nine years, but I grow weary. Enough to say that the mustard seed we had planted fifty years before had sprouted and put forth branches, and the birds of the air had come to rest in them. The birds are the tribes. Let me count them.

Among the first were the Chambas, the Verres and the Komas; then the Jukuns, Mumuyes and Bachamas; the Kilbas, Higis and Margis; the Pulkas, Ngamawa and Barres, and lastly, the Wajjas, the Mbulas and the Lallas. I bless them all. I love them all.

I was still a young lion. Age could not weary me. Instead of a horse I now drove a Beatle which I called my Blue Sister. She was loyal, very loyal. Swamps, sand, narrow bush paths, she balked at nothing. The first little boys whom we brought in and trained to become catechists, they strove mightily to evangelise their brothers. They are old and bent now, and I love them. Many of the sons of the old catechists became priests, and two of them are bishops.

Towards the end of these years, having more time for writing, I wrote twenty necessary books in English, ten in Hausa and a couple in Chamba and Margi, besides numerous hymns in all the languages. Books in English were: *Jesus Is My Saviour*, a large scriptural catechism; *The Story of the Church; Our Holy Mass;* and *Bread from Heaven*.

Then the Story of St Augustine, of St Monica, of St Francis, of St Antony, of the Little Flower, of the Uganda Martyrs and of the Mombasa Martyrs. After these came *The Real Mary, New Life in Christ* (the Sacraments), *Please Baptize my Child, Marriage in God, Lord Teach Me to Pray* and, last of all, *Are Catholics Stupid?*

Hausa is the lingua franca of about ten million people. I translated ten of these books into Hausa. Then, from the Latin, I did the *Sunday Mass Missal, The Ritual* and *The Adult Catechumenate*. My biggest job was a volume of *Sermons for the Sundays of the Three Year Cycle*. They are for the use of catechists, teachers and others who preside at the Sunday Service in bush chapels when there is no priest.

Do I seem to boast a little? Perhaps. But if I do not praise myself, who will? Besides, one must think of posterity, they deserve it! But my proudest boast, if you want to know, is that wherever I have lived, I have been loved. I did not deserve it, being three parts rascal, but I thank God for it just the same. As we know, of all the lovely things there are in life, the loveliest is to love, and to be loved.

In November '94 I celebrated my eightieth birthday. My bishop presided at a Thanksgiving Mass and praised me mightily. My people sang and danced for joy in my honour. I was still a young lion, with many years of action before me. But even lions must bow to time. In April '95 I was invalided home. 'And don't come back,' my bishop said.

Ah, well! All I said was, 'Othello's occupation's gone!'

Flying home, three miles up in the sky, I looked down on Nigeria and thought of the beginnings of fifty years ago, when travel was by horse and foot, when we swam the rivers, climbed the mountains, learned the languages and taught our people that God is a God of Love. Where we found only a handful of Christians, there are now three dioceses, Yola, Maiduguri and Jalingo. Besides, we founded the Order of St Augustine, which flourishes in Africa even as it declines in Ireland.

Praise God, I say, as I fly away. And his Mother. And the little Flower. It was, you may say, satisfactory.

7

OH, MY COUNTRY!

'All things betray thee who betrayest Me'

In April '95, then, I came home for good. The first thing I noticed as I walked the streets was how lithe young ladies overtook and passed me by with the greatest of ease. It made me rather sad. It was not always thus.

Waking up at 5.30 on my first morning home, I waited for the Angelus bells to ring, the innocent little convent bells of the Liberties. Once upon a time their bell-music used to float in with the cold morning air over the top of my window: the Holy Faith, the Presentation, the Mercy and the Charity. I waited in vain. The bells were silent.

Then I found that while I had been busy building a new Christendom in Africa, many of my own people had been deserting theirs. They had begun the long, slow, slide down into apostasy. Like lemmings they were migrating into a new and shrunken universe, a mental migration more deadly than any bodily one. The Light of the World was quenched and his wisdom spurned.

It pained me. It pains me every day. I hear the Voice mourning over his people as he mourned over the apostate Jews of long ago: 'Why have my people abandoned me, the fountain of living water, and dug for themselves cisterns, leaking cisterns that can hold no water?'

I hear the voice of Jesus mourning the little children for whom he died: 'Let the little children come to me and do not stop them, for the Kingdom of Heaven belongs to such as these.' But their faithless parents do stop them and they grow up to wander in the dark, ignorant of their Saviour and their God.

This new universe is, on the surface, full of life and rushing change, but its heart is dead. My universe, the one I grew up in, was a-tingle with the presence of God. Every flower lifted its innocent face and smiled, and whispered, 'He made me. Lots of me. He loves little things.'

Joseph Mary Plunkett could write:

> *I see his blood upon the rose,*
> *And in the stars the glory of his eyes;*
> *His body gleams amid eternal snows,*
> *His tears fall from the skies.*

We knew that we were immortal; that we came from God, belonged to God and would go to God. We knew that already we had Eternal Life, and were given the Bread from heaven to nourish it. We admitted that we were sinners, and cleansed our hearts in confession. We knew that our God had died of love and risen again, and that our destiny was to share forever in his love. He had a Mother who was our Mother too. We could turn to her for comfort in our hours of desolation.

All in all it was a warm universe. We were poor, yes, very poor, but rich in that we possessed God, and with him the riches of heaven. Today, old ladies say to me, 'When we were young we had nothing, but we were happy. Now they have everything and they're not happy.' It is the fashion today to deride that world because it was Catholic. Intolerant liberals desire to shepherd us all into the new and shrunken universe. They urge us to cut our roots, our religion and our history, thus to cease being a nation and to become a rabble without religion or honour. If they read *King Lear* they might heed Albany's warning to Lear's unnatural daughters. It holds for nations too:

> *She that herself will sliver and disbranch*
> *From her maternal sap, perforce must wither*
>   *And come to deadly use.*

Deadly use. We see it in our newspapers each morning. It is plain that the more we abandon our religion, the more savage we become. Newman truly wrote: 'We need the truths of religion to arrest fierce and wilful human nature on its onward course, and to rescue it from its suicidal excesses.'

Why then do so many desire that the Catholic Church should perish from the earth? Jesus himself told his disciples, 'You will be hated by all nations on account of my name.'

But why? Hilaire Belloc gives a partial answer: 'One thing in this world is different from all other. It has a personality and a force. It is recognised and, [when recognised], most violently loved or hated. It is the Catholic Church. Within that household the human spirit has roof and hearth. Outside, it is night.'

When Jesus came into the world we crucified him. Our new world bristles at any hint of his return. Away with him! The Catholic Church claims to be his living Body. Away with her! Like Indians galloping around the covered waggons, so her enemies circle the Church, bang-banging gaily, riding high, wide and handsome. May they not be riding a little recklessly? After all, a Man did die on a Cross. And for them. Why? For love, infinite love. So that the sins of all of us might be forgiven. It was written of him in prophecy five hundred years before he came:

> *Ours were the sufferings he bore,*
> *Ours the sorrows he carried.*
> *For our faults he was pierced,*
> *crushed for our sins,*
> *and through his wounds we are healed.*

Was he not mad to die for us? Yes, divinely mad. As he hung on the Cross his arms were flung wide, calling us to himself, while his blood, dripping, lay in a pool on the ground. Of that blood St Augustine wrote: 'The blood of Christ, if you wish, was shed for you; if you do not wish, it was not shed for you.'

We are free to say Yes or No. Jesus leaves us free – and responsible. It is sad to hear ladies murmur, 'I was brought up a Catholic – the nuns, you know. But I no longer find religion relevant.'

Religion not relevant? 'You must love the Lord your God with all your heart, and your neighbour as yourself.' Not relevant to our deadly world?

'You must not steal' – in any of the ways of chicanery, fraud, misuse of public monies. Not relevant?

'You must not commit adultery.' Well . . .

'You must not kill.' Is it not relevant to the child in the womb? *'You must not kill me!'* The fact is that we find religion too, too relevant, and try to sweep it under the carpet.

Is God necessary?

But is God really necessary? Can we not jog along comfortably without any Christ, any religion? Many people believe we can. Blaise Pascal, the French philosopher, doubts it: 'We may say that without Christ, we understand nothing whatever of our life or death, of man or of God. . . . When men try to live without God, they either imagine themselves to be God and go mad, or become animals.'

We have seen it happen. The clever Europeans of the last century were sure that they had killed God. Nietzsche, the German inventor of the Superman, sprang into the pulpit to preach the Funeral Oration of God: 'Where is God? I'll tell you. We have killed him, you and I. Can't you hear the sound of the grave-diggers who are burying God? God is dead! He was entirely superfluous. Never was there so great a deed. We have freed men from God!'

Great stuff! Now it happened that in 1854 Pope Pius IX proclaimed the fact of the Immaculate Conception of Mary: 'that, from the first moment of her conception . . . by virtue of the merits of Jesus Christ . . . Mary was preserved immune from all stain of original sin.' The whole tribe of liberals and their toadies burst their sides laughing. Poor old Pope! Poor old Catholic Church! Don't they know yet that God is dead? Ha ha ha!

Then, while they were still giggling and gloating, the thing happened. Gently as falling dew it happened. The little girl went out to gather a bundle of sticks for the fire, and met the Mother of God. Not once, but many times. The priest, sceptical, told her, 'Ask the lady her name.' She did, and the Lady replied, 'I am the Immaculate Conception.'

There was no doubt about it. All France rang with the news. The real, old-fashioned miracles were happening again! The Empress herself came to pray!

'But it's impossible! God is dead.'

'But it's happening. Come and see.'

Charcot of Paris, the eminent neurologist, celebrated by Axel Munthe in *San Michele,* was invited. He refused to come. Zola came and saw a girl just cured of lupus, the skin of whose face was still red and raw. 'How ugly!' he muttered, and walked away.

These fellows who were so good at killing God ran away when confronted by a simple miracle. Their trouble was heart-disease, the kind that affects the brain. King David sang in a psalm 3,000 years ago, 'The *fool* hath said in his heart, "There is no God."' In his heart, note, not in his head; a conclusion of wishful thinking, not of reasoning. People simply don't want God. As Malcolm Muggeridge remarked of his atheistic days, 'I refused to admit the existence of a personal God, because I felt that he might severely limit the personal activities of M. Muggeridge.'

We don't want God; we want a good-bad time. We try to live without God, then, as Pascal says, we imagine ourselves to be God and go mad. We become, not a-theists but Auto-theists, arbiters of what is good and what is evil. We may even decree that it is lawful to kill our infants in the womb.

Modern folk are indeed a perverse lot. When they find a watch ticking away they conclude it had a maker. When they find the infinitely more complex universe ticking away, they deny that it had a Maker! Yet the greatest and the smallest things cry aloud the Name of God. The countless galaxies, hurtling on their ordered courses through infinite space, show the powerful Reason that holds the universe together; the tiny cell and the primordial units of life reveal the same Reason. We are forced to say, with St Bonaventure: 'The man who does not see here is blind, and the man who does not hear is deaf. The man who does not begin to adore here and refuses to praise the creating Intelligence, is dumb.'

'What will happen?'

If God is dead, does it really matter? Was he not superfluous after all? What difference does his departure make? Nietzsche himself, having preached God's Funeral Oration, gives us the startling answer:

> The fact that faith in a Christian God is dying, is already casting its first shadows over Europe. Many people do not realise what will fall into ruin now that the Faith is undermined, this Faith which was the foundation of the whole scheme of European ethics. We must henceforth expect a long series of demolitions,

destructions, ruins and combustions, such immense terrors, such darkness and eclipse as men have never known.

They have come, the darkness and the terrors. We have reached the end of the bloodiest and most brutal century in history – two murderous World Wars, a host of lesser wars, the planned extermination of a whole people, the general slaughter of infants in the womb, sexual 'freedom' that ends in disillusion and bitterness, and, worst of all, the crumbling of the family, which means the crumbling of society and the end of civilisation.

It is plain that our only hope is to kneel again before the One who said, 'I am the Way, and the Truth and the Life. . . . Without Me you can do nothing.' We have broken with him and, like a dislocated arm, we are in pain until we are relocated. Are we in any way guilty of our apostasy? Well, Jesus did say, 'This is the judgement, that the Light has come into the world, but men loved darkness rather than light, because their deeds were evil.'

Punishment?
There are prophets who predict that God is about to punish the world. But no, God does not lift his hand to smite. But he may allow the evil that is in us to run its logical course to disaster. The apostasy of the Jews in 600 BC led to their captivity in Babylon. Their rejection of Christ himself when he came led to the destruction of their nation. Sin brings its own punishment. The sober words of Teilhard de Chardin stand: 'The day is not far distant when humanity will realise that, biologically, it is faced with a choice between suicide and adoration.'

The words of Malraux, quoted by Pope John Paul, echo Teilhard: 'The 21st century will be a century of religion, or it will not be at all.' It is later than we think. It is high time we faced up to the only really important questions in life: Whence? Why? Whither? Where did I come from? Why am I here? Where do I go from here? When I ask young people, 'Why did God make you?' they just gawk. Yet the answer is there on the first page of the catechism: 'God made me to know him, to love him, to serve him in this world, and to be happy with him forever in heaven.'

We foolish fools imagine we have outgrown the wisdom of the catechism. We bury our faces in the picture-box, our anaesthetic against thought. Meanwhile, like lemmings, we move imperceptibly to the edge of eternity and, day by day, one by one, fall over. We have a choice – to fall into the arms of a loving God, or into the abyss.

Like it or not, we are immortal. As C. S. Lewis wrote: 'We are all immortal. All the people around us are immortal. All are destined to become immortal gods and goddesses, or immortal horrors such as one meets in a nightmare.'

Day by day we manufacture ourselves, what we shall be hereafter. May Jesus in his mercy save us.

The Shadowy Companion

One wonders has Satan anything to do with our sweeping rejection of Christ? It has become fashionable to say, 'Thank God (!) we live in a sanitised universe – No God, no devil, no spirits good or bad.'

A guru of the radio assures us that 'the devil is only an invention of Irish parish priests to frighten their flocks'. God bless his innocence! Jesus told the Jews: 'The devil was a murderer from the beginning . . . . He is a liar, and the father of all lies.' He is 'the Prince of this world'.

Kenneth Clarke, he of the *Civilization* series, says: 'We cannot discount the activity of that Shadowy Companion who is always with us, like an inverted Guardian Angel, silent, invisible, almost incredible – yet unquestionably there.'

André Gide, the famous French novelist, gives us an anguished account of the devil's activity. Gide grew up a pious Protestant youth. As a young man he went to Algeria, where he met Oscar Wilde. 'Wilde,' he said, 'seduced me.' In 1916 a glance from Christ pierced him. He records it in his diary, *Numquid Et Tu?*

> *23 April.* Terrible filth, the filth of sin: Ashes left by an impure flame. Can you not cleanse me of it, Lord? That with your help I may again sing your praise?

> *16 June.* I can no longer pray, no longer even hear God. I now despair of my own wisdom, and when I lack the joy that he

gives, I have no other. You should come, Lord. Let not the Evil One take your place in my heart. If you leave me, he makes his home there.

19 Sept. The storm has raged all night. I get up, with brain and heart empty, laden with the entire weight of hell. If I could only relate this drama, depict Satan as he is when he has taken possession of a man, could relate how he makes use of him to influence others. An absurd notion, you may think. But I have lately understood it for the first time.

You are not merely taken prisoner, *but the evil which is an active power demands from you activity in its service. You are compelled to fight in a false and perverse cause.*

That is a chilling thought for the people of the media who have the power to mould peoples' minds and hearts.

In ancient days devils took open possession of people and were recognised for what they were. In this more sophisticated age their ploy is to pretend that they do not exist. Thus they can possess and use people without their being aware of it. More than ever, now, we need the prayer that we used to pray after Mass: 'Blessed Michael the Archangel, defend us in the hour of battle. Be our safeguard against the wickedness and snares of the devil . . .'

Lord Macaulay
An English tabloid announced gleefully: 'The game is up for the Catholic Church in Ireland.'

Really? Lord Macaulay, the historian, writing about the Church in the last century, would hardly agree. Being a stout Protestant, he felt he had to call the Church 'a work of human policy' – the one thing she is not. If she were, she should have perished long ago under the weight of scandals, wars and heresies. That she did not is because her Founder promised, 'Behold, I am with you always, yes, to the end of time.'

But let's hear Macaulay. It is a delightful piece of rhetoric:

There is not, and there never has been, a work of human policy so well deserving examination as the Catholic Church. The history of that Church joins together the two great ages of civilization. No other institution is left standing which carries the mind back to the time when the smoke of sacrifice rose from the Pantheon, and when camelopards bounded in the Flavian amphitheatre.

The proudest royal houses are but of yesterday, when compared to the line of the Supreme Pontiffs. That line we trace back in an unbroken series, from the Pope who crowned Napoleon in the 19th century, to the Pope who crowned Pepin in the 8th. The Republic of Venice was next in antiquity, but the Republic of Venice is gone, and the Papacy remains. The Papacy remains, not in decay, not an antique, but full of life and youthful vigour.

The Catholic Church is still sending forth to the ends of the earth missionaries as zealous as those who landed in Kent with Augustine, and is still confronting hostile Kings with the same spirit as she confronted Attila. Nor do we see any signs that the term of her long dominion is approaching. She saw the commencement of all the Governments and all the ecclesiastical establishments that now exist in the world; and we feel no assurance that she is not destined to see the end of them all. She was great and respected before the Saxon set foot in Britain, before the Frank had crossed the Rhine, when Grecian eloquence still flourished in Antioch, when idols were still worshipped in the temple of Mecca. And she may still exist in undiminished vigour when some traveller from New Zealand shall, in the midst of a vast solitude, take his stand on a broken arch of London Bridge to sketch the ruins of St Paul's.

Thank you, Macaulay. The Church endures because she is divine; she sins because she is human. She is a Church of sinners, and for sinners; her *raison d'être* is to offer salvation to sinners. If sinners deny they have sinned, she can do nothing for them. Her Head is Jesus, the Son of God, who came to save. Her members are grafted on to him by their baptism, which gives them a share in his divine life. The Head and members form one body, and the Holy Spirit, dwelling in the heart of each living member, is the soul of that body, sending the same divine life pulsing through every vein.

And the Heart of that body? It is the Blessed Eucharist, the Mass. There we come together, daily if we can, to eat and drink of divine Life and Love.

Let us Rejoice!

Let's rejoice then, we Catholics, for our Church is ever ancient, ever new, ever living because of Jesus and his Spirit. The Spirit first came upon her in the storm and fire of Pentecost. Storm and fire can still erupt unexpectedly. As Chesterton put it in *The Everlasting Man*, 'In the Church we still see those headlong acts of holiness that speak of something rapid and recent that startles the world like a suicide. But it is not a suicide; it is not pessimistic; it is still as optimistic as St Francis of the birds and flowers.' Or as optimistic, as headlong, as Mother Teresa of Calcutta and her legion of devoted Sisters, blessed ones whom to see is to see the work of the Spirit made plain.

Yes, in spite of begrudgers, we Catholics should lift our hearts and sing. In this Western world our numbers decrease, but the remnant is purer, holier and therefore more powerful than the numbers of old. The grace of one believer outweighs the emptiness of the many.

Even in our sadness let's rejoice, like St Peter, when his flock was being persecuted and a Cross was being got ready for himself! He tells them: 'On the Day when Jesus is revealed, you will win praise and glory. You do not see him, yet you love him, and, still without seeing him, you are filled with a joy so glorious that it cannot be expressed, because you believe, and are sure, of the salvation of your souls.'

Paul, too, rejoices in his sufferings. As they prepared to cut off his head he wrote: 'If God is for us, who can be against us? . . . Nothing can come between us and the love of Christ. . . . I am certain of this: neither death nor life, no angel, no prince, nothing that exists, nothing still to come, not any power, or height or depth, nor any created thing, can ever come between us and the love of God made visible in Christ Jesus our Lord.'

The Lord himself said simply: 'Can a mother forget the child at her breast? . . . Even if she can, I can never forget you. . . . I have loved you with an everlasting love.'

Best of all is this little psalm that sings:

> *Cry out with joy to God, all the earth,*
> *Serve the Lord with gladness.*
> *Come before him singing for joy.*

Away then with the poor mouth! Let's lift our hearts and sing. Sing and dance. We know the Way and the Truth, and we have the Life. The Way, the Truth and the Life are one Person who is Love of all love, Beauty of all beauty, and whose name is Jesus. Let's laugh and sing then. I tell the saints who come to confession, 'Rejoice! Be happy! You have your two feet on the road to heaven. Let the sky fall down and you don't care. Go home now and dance a jig on the kitchen floor.'

Then they laugh with delight. Yes, no matter how dark the day, the Light of the World is with us.

Wandering Hearts

I write this page for any young wanderer who may chance to read it:

If I were young again and had wandered away from my Saviour – had 'lost the Faith', as they say – the experience of a young Frenchman might help me find my way back.

Captain Charles de Foucauld belonged to an old Catholic military family. Posted to Algeria in 1890, he filled his nights with wine, women and song and was cashiered. To recover his honour, he went into the Sahara disguised as an Arab. For years he travelled up and down, mapping the territory and gathering intelligence on the tribes for his Government.

He came home a national hero. But his sister was not impressed. 'You have abandoned your ancestral faith,' she said. 'Without it you are nothing. Go and see the Abbé Huvelin' – a family friend. He protested. She insisted. To please her he went, and said to the priest, 'Father, I have come only because of my sister. But it's no use. I no longer believe.'

'Kneel down and confess your sins,' said the priest.

'But I tell you, I did not come for that.'

'Kneel down and confess.'

'But I tell you, I have not the Faith.'

'You know your desert wells,' said the priest. 'Choked with sand. Apparently dry. Yet there is sweet water deep down. Dig, and you find it. It's the same with you. You were baptised. Deep in your soul some of the sweet waters of the Faith remain, covered over with the debris of sin. Dig! Confess, and you will find it.'

Like a man in a dream the soldier dropped on his knees and made a full confession of his life. He buried his face in his hands then and began to sob like a child. It was the little child who is buried in every person, breaking through the hard crust, released. He went straight to Holy Communion. After that he wanted God and God only. He became a priest and returned to the desert to minister to the French soldiers there. Finally, desiring to be alone with God, he built himself a stone hermitage at Tamanrasset, high on the Hoggar Plateau, where he adored the Blessed Sacrament until, in 1917, a marauding band of Tuaregs killed him.

You say you have lost your faith? Now you know how to get it back. Have you the courage of the soldier? Your faith is there, buried deep under the debris of the years. Dig and you will find it. Dig on your knees!

The Questions They Ask!

They are brash, the youngsters of today. The questions they ask! In my day we would have called them cheeky and slapped them down. But these ones are earnest and demand straight answers.

'Kevin, were you ever sorry for being a priest?'

'No, thank God. Not for a moment, nor half a moment. I always knew that to be near God and to do his work was for me the happiest thing.'

'Did you ever fall in love?'

'Not since I was thirteen.'

'People think that because you are celibate you are anti-woman.'

'What, me! My son, I have adored all women since I was a boy – well, nearly all!'

'But were you ever attracted to women?'

'But naturally! I have met many a blue-eyed smile, and smiled again.'

'But was there ever any special, special one?'

'Well, possibly, one or two who resembled Antoine de Saint-Exupery's famous lass. He wrote of her: "The woman I have in mind could, with her smile, build up for you, effortlessly, an inimitable masterpiece, and by grace of witnessing that smile, one dwelt for a moment in a world of shining peace and love's eternity."' Yes, I have known one or two such, and touched them with my heart. But by God's grace I kept myself to myself. I felt no need to tie myself to the mast like Odysseus when the Sirens sang their song!'

'But why don't priests get married if they want to?'

'Because it's a law of our Church. That's why.'

'I think celibacy is silly.'

'Do you? If I had a wife and kids do you think I could have gone about the world on my Master's business as I did? Celibacy leaves a man free to give himself completely to Christ and his work. He can love and serve a thousand families instead of one.'

'But it's not *natural!*'

'No, it's *supernatural.* What you people don't understand is that celibacy is a call from God, and a gift from God. When he calls a man he gives him the necessary grace to live out his commitment . . . Mind you, to have a wife and children is a lovely thing. But to give them up for the sake of Christ is lovelier still. If you want to know, it is the noblest sacrifice a man or woman can offer to God. After martyrdom.'

'But do you think God wants you to make this huge sacrifice?'

'I do, for Jesus said, "There are people who have renounced marriage for the sake of the Kingdom of Heaven. Let anyone accept this who can." The priest accepts the challenge.'

'Did you ever, even once, wish to marry?'

'No, I did not. You see, I am not my own man. I am an ordained man. I belong to Christ. He consecrated me to carry out the most sacred action on earth.'

'What's that?'

'The Mass, of course. The Son of God still offering himself in sacrifice to his heavenly Father for the salvation of the world.'

'But could you not do that even if you were married?'

'Certainly. But in the days when the martyrs still bled in the Colosseum, men felt instinctively that those who handled the sacred things of God ought not marry. In the beginning there were married priests and bishops. But the ideal of celibacy gradually spread among them. You see, in those days Christians were, you may say, dazzled by the virginity of Jesus and Mary. They wanted to imitate them, just as you want to be like your pop stars. Celibacy gradually became the custom, and after three hundred years it became law in the Catholic Church.'

'All the same, I think it's cruel.'

'My dear, remember that I was twenty-five when I was ordained. There was no compulsion whatever. It was my own free choice.'

'But, Kevin, can't you see that unless you have married priests you will soon have no priests at all.'

'Yes, I have heard that cry: "Abolish celibacy and you will have plenty of vocations." Moryah! Young people are drawn to what is hard and heroic, not to what is soft. The Holy Spirit still calls. Mark my words: in due course the best of young men and women will turn away from the pigswill of lust, money and selfishness, which is all the world offers them. They will seek truth and sacrifice again in Jesus Christ. I wouldn't be surprised if some of you were among them!'

'What? Us! Kevin, you must be mad!'

'Kevin, where were you born?'

'In Enniscorthy town,' I tell them. 'In 1914, Nurse Pierce delivered me, (I remember!) She gave me the necessary smack, and within a year I had won First Prize as the Bonniest Baby of the County Wexford.'

'Oh, Kevin, you must have been gorgeous!'

'Maybe, but my mother said it was because all the other bonnie babies were wailing, whereas I was laughing and grabbing at the nurses who unveiled my beauty.'

The brash ones have had enough. They depart. I am left alone. But I know that to the end of time, men and women will be found to give up all for the sake of Him who gave up all for them. They will join the army that has marched down history for two thousand years, stripped for action, the perennial strength and glory of the Catholic Church.

Agnes the Martyr shows the way: 'All the world and its allurements I have despised for the sake of my Lord Jesus Christ, whom I have loved, in whom I have believed, whom I have chosen.'

We Priests

By our falls, we priests have hurt and shocked our people. We have given many an excuse to abandon their religion. Not a logical reaction, when you think that one of the Twelve trained by Jesus himself betrayed him, yet no disciples made Judas an excuse for abandoning Jesus.

Jesus said, 'Go out and teach all nations.' Since then, thousands of his messengers have gone out each year. Is it any wonder that some should stumble and fall? Why point at the soldiers who fall out, and ignore the Army that marches on?

To be a priest in these times is hard. Some people detest us. Many are coldly indifferent. We feel unwanted, unnecessary; we are tempted to lose heart and to abandon our faithless people. It is a temptation Jesus must have felt when his own people rejected him. How ought we handle it? Fyodor Dostoevsky, the Russian writer, points the way:

> If the people around you are spiteful and callous and will not hear you, fall down before them and beg their forgiveness, for in truth you are to blame for their not wanting to hear you. And if you cannot speak to them in their bitterness, serve them in silence and in humility, never losing hope. If all men abandon you, and even drive you away by force, then, when you are left alone, fall on the earth and kiss it; water it with your tears and it will bring forth fruit, even though no one has heard you or seen you in your solitude.
>
> Believe to the end, even if all men went astray and you were left the only one faithful; bring your offering even then and praise God in your loneliness. And if two of you are gathered together – then there is a whole world, a world of living love. Embrace each other tenderly and praise God, for, if only in the two of you, His truth has been fulfilled.
>
> From *The Brothers Karamazov*

We priests, as long as we cling to Christ and his Mass, we are invincible.

8

AND MUST I DIE?

Roots

A man nearing his end tends to hark back to his roots. In the year 1998 I revisited the town of my birth, and sat on the bridge over the Slaney at the foot of Vinegar Hill. I had crossed this bridge every day during my earliest schooldays, climbing the hill to the Convent of Mercy with other little boys and girls. Where are they? And the thousands of men and women, so vital then, bustling about their business – all silent, vanished into the earth. All gone!

I move to the cemetery, 'the plain of crosses', where they rest. So much passion lies buried here! The loves and hates, the joys and sorrows, the broken hearts, the angers, all quenched in eternity. I stand over the graves of my own people and whisper their names one by one – Father, Mother, my beloved brother Dermot and sisters Mairead and Eimer, the aunt who said 'Buff will be the priest', Margaret, the youngest of the Three Handsome Pierces, and Willie Purcell, singer of songs, whom she loved in 1866. I pray to them and say goodbye.

Coming away, I hear the tap of a drum. The Wexfordmen are marching today to commemorate the courage and death of their ancestors in 1798. I see them come, three thousand strong, pikes aloft, dressed like their ancestors in white shirts, black waistcoats and trousers gathered at the knee. They come, three abreast, serious, disciplined, solemn, and a lump rises in my throat. The ghosts of two of my ancestors march with them.

Today Mass will be offered for the souls of the Wexfordmen who fell in battle in the counties Carlow, Kildare, Meath and Dublin. They lie in unmarked graves, buried where they fell. I see the banners of the people of those counties, come to do them honour. The people of Ballyboughal are here – Baile Baculi, the Town of the Staff, where St Patrick's crozier was treasured for over a thousand years. It was here that the last of the Wexfordmen fell.

We offer solemn Mass for their souls. The Last Post is sounded and a high Celtic Cross unveiled. I set out for home, thanking God that the people of Wexford have not betrayed their history or their Faith.

And must I really die?

Yes, thank God. Who could endure life-without-end in this mad world? And must I fear to die? No, thank God, for God is pity and love, and death is a Shining Door. I must pass through it to meet Jesus face to face – he who is beauty of all beauty, love of all love, my Saviour and my God. To gaze on him face to face, to be drowned in him, that is the essence of heaven.

Face to face, too, I shall gaze into the eyes of his Mother, the Morning Star, fair as the moon, bright as the sun, possessing in herself all beauty, all love, all tenderness. I think it is she, his Mother and ours, who will wipe away all tears from our eyes when we come through the shining door.

Socrates, wisest of men, said that a wise person will rehearse his death. As I write, I am rehearsing my own death, so that when the bell tolls I may not panic, but lay me down in peace. Being an odd fellow, I take comfort from a line in Shakespeare's *Henry IV*, Part I. The rascally Falstaff is going about, pressing men into the King's army. Those who can bribe him go free. Poor little Feeble, a woman's tailor by trade, can pay no bribe, so soldier he must. All he said was:

> By my troth I care not!
> A man can die but once;
> We owe God a death.

We owe God a death! It takes Shakespeare to throw off a line like that, simple and profound. It says, in effect, 'You died for me, Lord, so I owe you. Since I must die, let my death be a repayment for yours. Whatever pain and humiliation may come, I offer it to you for yours, even now.'

Another word that gives me comfort was spoken by Leon Bloy, the eccentric French Catholic writer. As he lay dying, his friend Maritain asked him, 'What do you feel now, Leon, at the edge of eternity?'

'An immense curiosity,' said Bloy.

That is how I should like to feel; no fear, only curiosity about what my Lord has prepared for me, my Lord who loves me. Soon my soul must come trembling out of its stronghold, this warm body that has been its home for so long. Am I afraid? Not in the least. Why? Because I have no sins? Don't be silly! I have sinned, but I have repented and been forgiven. It is because I know what God is like. He told us what he is like, gave us a complete character sketch of himself in a short story.

What God is Like

A man had two sons, Jesus said. The younger said to his father, 'Father, give me my share of the property.' In effect he is saying, 'Give it to me now – I'll get it anyway when you're dead – and let me get out of here.'

Very good; the father gave him his share. The boy turned it into cash, packed up and went away 'to a far country'. No affection, no love. A callous, hard-hearted lad. He got what he wanted, a good-bad time while his money lasted. Then the famine, the hunger, the thought of home.

Then Jesus said, 'At last he came to his senses,' implying that the man who turns his back on God is out of his senses. The boy said, 'I will leave this place and go back to my father and say, "Father, I have sinned against heaven and against you. I am not worthy to be called your son."'

He set out for home, barefoot, emaciated, in rags. Now comes the nub of the story. How will his father receive him? Jesus tells us: 'While he was still *a long way off* his father saw him' – he had evidently been watching the road, longing for his son's return.

'His heart was filled with pity' – pity, not anger and condemnation. 'He ran to him, threw his arms around him and kissed him' – eager, loving, full of joy. The boy began to stammer out his confession, 'Father, I have sinned. I am not worthy.'

But the father called out to his servants, 'Hurry! Bring the best gown and put it on him. Put a ring on his finger and shoes on his feet. Kill the fatted calf and let's have a feast. For this son of mine was dead and has come alive; was lost and is found.'

Then they began the feast, with music and dance and song. And that, Jesus is telling us, is how God welcomes back the poor, sad, repentant sinner. That, he tells us, is what God is like. And he should know, being himself God.

So, when my poor soul comes trembling out of its stronghold, my soul, my essential self, my 'I', and a rascally 'I' at that, bearing the scars of many a sin – when, I say, I come forth and stand shivering, lost, by the strange cold sea of eternity – what then? Why, he who loves me will see me from afar, his heart will be filled with pity, he will run to me and hug me. I shall see him as he is, dimly or in a dazzling flash. Perhaps I shall stammer out, 'Jesus, I'm sorry . . .'

But he will command the younger angels, 'Hurry! Glorify him! Beautify him! Put a celestial gown on him! And let's have a feast, for this is my dear son's first day in heaven.'

And then the Party! My Party, when all my loved ones will gather round me; my dear, dear ones so long parted, with music and song and dance – a celestial disco that goes on and on! And then the talk, the loving talk that will never end.

'But what of Purgatory?'

Yes, I jumped the gun, didn't I, in my eagerness to breast the tape! Purgatory – it means purification. Thank God for it, for I need to be purified. I dare not join the company of the Holy Ones as I am. Though I have repented, the roots of my old sins remain, my pride, covetousness, lust and anger. Above all, my lack of love. For I have been like flint to some I did not like. I have let loose my anger and scarified those who were weaker than I. Worst, I have been hard-hearted and withheld love from those who most needed it. I am like an old plank, full of the knots and warps I have built into myself. I am in need of deep, deep healing.

Who will be my healer? Who but the Holy Spirit, the Spirit of Love, my psychiatrist, my loving soul-doctor. Softly, softly, he will unravel the knots and warps, and expand my heart to be able to receive, and to give perfect love. Then the gentle voice, 'Come to Me.'

But what of the *pain* of Purgatory? Well, yes, there is pain, but not the kind you imagine. My God will not say to me, 'K. Cullen, you've been a bad boy. Ten years in the fire for you.'

Ah, no! God is not like that. My pain will consist in my being held back from him for a time. I have glimpsed him from afar. I am made for him. My whole being longs for him, yearns for him, pants for him, cries out for him, thirsts for him like a man dying of thirst in the desert. I burn with love and longing for him, and that is the fire of Purgatory. But I am held back. But the prayers of my loved ones on earth are helping me. Above all, the sweet Sacrifice of the Mass. Like rain on the desert they fall on my soul. Then, at last – ah, the ecstasy! The release of the bent bow! The flight of the arrow into the heart of my God.

It will be, you may say, satisfactory!

There are scholars who say that all this happens in a split second. It may be so. But I prefer it in slow motion!

'Will I know my loved ones?'

I ask, will it be heaven if you do not? As I said before, in Deansgrange Cemetery, Dublin, there stands a headstone that bears one word only, carved large and deep into the stone: MAMMY. The cry of love and anguish from some mother's son! I ask, will it be heaven for him if he does not meet his Mammy and lay his head on her breast once more?

I once accompanied a friend to visit his wife in the Hospice for the Dying. As we parted she called out to him, 'Remember, Séamus, I love you from here to eternity.' They were her last words. That night she died. Shall they not love each other with a perfect love, now that they are made perfect in heaven?

Yes, we shall meet our loved ones again, and rejoice with them. And talk about why God in his wisdom allowed this and that to happen, and drop a tear, maybe, for old, unhappy, far-off things, and forgive, and ask forgiveness. Yes, that I should like; that I long for, to ask forgiveness of all I ever hurt, and they are many. St Paul, long after his conversion, was haunted by the memory of the Christians he had persecuted. 'When they were put to death,' he tells us in the Acts, 'I cast my vote against them.' He took part in the lynching of St Stephen. A poet imagines Paul meeting those saints in heaven:

Saint, did I say? With your remembered faces,
Dear men and women whom I sought and slew!

Ah, when we mingle in the heavenly places
How I shall weep to Stephen and to you!
So true, so true! To weep to hearts we have hurt will give us
heart's-ease at last.

'What of our bodies?'

Well, 'I believe in the resurrection of the body'. Finish!

The fact is that these mortal bodies of ours, dead and turned to
clay, will, on the last day, rise glorious and beautiful, subtle and
impassible, bright and immortal – not the heavy, dense lumps of
matter they are now. St Paul guarantees it: 'The Lord Jesus Christ will
transfigure these wretched bodies of ours into copies of his own
glorious body,' as he revealed it in the Transfiguration.

So my risen body will not be a reproduction of my old one, now so
old and tired. It will be utterly changed, made spiritual and immortal,
at home in a glorified and immortal universe. Paul tells us: 'The body
that is buried is mortal, it will be raised up immortal; buried as a
physical body, it will be raised up a spiritual body.' Then he gives a cry
of joy: 'And when this perishable nature has put on imperishability
and this mortal has put on immortality, then shall come to pass the
saying that is written, "Death is swallowed up in victory". O Death,
where is thy sting? O Grave, where is thy victory?'

Praise God! Mary has gone before us in an anticipated resurrection.
The Woman of Destiny, the sinless one who clothed her God in her
own flesh and blood, who was his comrade in suffering and in saving
us, the only one of us who never had a sin to repent – why should she
wait? Where she has gone, in her radiant and immortal flesh, we shall
follow. We shall gaze into her eyes, she who is utterly human and
utterly heavenly, our innocent little sister and our mother. With her we
shall feel utterly at home.

The Heart of the Lamb

St John tells us that 'we shall be like Christ, because we shall see him
as he is'. I feel we may be surprised to find how perfectly human he is.
When John the Baptist saw him walking along the riverbank he cried
out, 'Look, there is the Lamb of God; there is he who takes away the

sin of the world.' Lamb! Not Lion of God but *lamb*, gentlest of all creatures and symbol of innocence.

Paul Claudel, the distinguished French diplomat and writer, gives us precious insight into the heart of the Lamb. Claudel was baptised as an infant but grew up an unbeliever, blasé and self-sufficient. One Easter Sunday he drifted into the church of Notre Dame, not to pray but to hear the choir sing vespers. They were singing the *Magnificat*, Mary's song of joy, when – but let him speak for himself:

> Then the event took place which dominates all my life. In an instant my heart was touched and I believed. I believed with such a clinging force, such an uprising of my whole being, with so powerful a conviction, that since then all the books, reasonings and arguments, all the hazards of an agitated life have not been able to shake my faith. Suddenly I was lacerated by an impression of the innocence, of the eternal childhood of God, a revelation never to be blotted out.

The innocence . . . the eternal childhood of God . . . An insight to brood over, that the All-powerful, the Creator and Sustainer has the heart of an innocent child; a heart that can be hurt and weep tears; that can cry out, 'Reproach has broken my heart. I looked for compassion but found none. In my thirst they gave me vinegar to drink.'

It is a glimpse into the Mystery at the heart of things. Given such childlike innocence, what man or woman, isolated from God, can hesitate to turn back to him?

Farewell!

My twilight hour has come. It is eighty-five years since I was the Bonniest Baby of the County Wexford. I am near the Shining Door. I write down for myself these bits and scraps that take my fancy and lift my heart.

The first is from a psalm King David wrote one thousand years before Christ:

> What have I in heaven but you?
> My happiness lies in you alone.

> Apart from you I have nothing on earth.
> My body and my heart faint for you;
> God is my possession forever.
> To be near God is my happiness.

Yes, in my life I have found it to be so. To be near him is my happiness, to be far away is my sadness.

Then, to suit my mood, there is this prayer of summer-twilight-peace from Cardinal Newman:

> May he support us all the day long, till the shades lengthen and evening comes, and the busy world is hushed, and the fever of life is over and our work is done. Then, in his mercy, may he give us a safe lodging, and a holy rest, and peace at last.

To that I say Amen! And again Amen!

I love, too, Peig Sayers, lovely valediction to life, translated from the Gaelic:

> But now my life is spent, as a candle, and my hope is rising every day that I'll be called into the eternal kingdom. May God guide me on this long road I have not travelled before. I think, now, everything is folly except for loving God.

True for you, Peig. May He give us the wisdom to know it.

Last and loveliest, these dying words of St Teresa of Avila, the great Spanish mystic: 'My Beloved, it is time for us to see each other.' In other words, for long enough we've been talking by long-distance telephone. Don't you think it is time we met face to face?

Only now, at at the very end, do I realise how human is the God who became man for me – how homely and friendly.

I am an ex-sinner: I have sinned, repented, confessed and been forgiven, so I have a strong, strong hope that I may come to heaven's gate. I may hesitate there, as who would not? But he who loves me will call out, 'Come on in, Kev. Don't be shy. It was for this that I suffered and died, just so you and I might live together always. Come in and meet my Mother. She's expecting you.'

Then she who loves me, she whose smile dazzles heaven and earth, will smile on me – on me! – and the bliss of that smile will thrill my heart for eternity.

Yes, it will be, you may say, satisfactory!